According to Festus

According to Festus

PROFOUND WORDS OF WISDOM BY
FESTUS HAGGEN OF GUNSMOKE©
FAME WITH SUPPORTING
BIBLICAL PROVERBS

―⸺

Richard L. Hamilton

Copyright© 2016 Richard L. Hamilton
All rights reserved
ISBN-13: 9781534713970
ISBN-10: 1534713972

Other publications by the author available on *Amazon* are:

Oh Hast Thou Forgotten, Michigan Cavalry in the Civil War: The Gettysburg Campaign. (2008).

The Plant, Oh Quality Where Art Thou: The Culture of General Motors. (2009).

Shiloh to Durham Station: 18th Wisconsin Infantry Regiment, With Captain Robert S. McMichael's Civil War Letters. (2010).

A Man From Montana: Memoirs of My Life in Western Montana, by Freeman A. Halverson. (Edited 2011).

Pals Forever: Memoirs of a Labrador in His Own Words. (2012).

Dearest Lydia: 1856-1864 Courtship & Civil War Letters From George T. & Lydia Ann Denton-Patten With Letters From Family and Friends. (2016).

To Ruth Ann, my wife, my love, my friend, and pal forever, and to our son Brad who loves to tell and hear a good humorous story.

To David Otto my turkey farmer friend of Middleville, Michigan who has said that a turkey is the smartest bird known to man, but it only knows two things; where it is not supposed to be, and how to get there.

Table of Contents

Acknowledgement · xv
Foreword · xvii
Preface · xxi
Prelude · xxiii

Chapter 1   Festus' Sayings · · · · · · · · · · · · · · · · · 1
Chapter 2   Festus' Conversations & Encounters With
               Supporting Proverbs & Bible Passages · · · · · · 95

     1. Falsely Accused · · · · · · · · · · · · · · · · 95
     2. Ex-Convict, Phoenix · · · · · · · · · · · · · · 99
     3. Miss Tara · · · · · · · · · · · · · · · · · · · 100
     4. Miss Phoebe · · · · · · · · · · · · · · · · · · 101
     5. Festus, Square Dance Caller · · · · · · · · · · 102
     6. Festus Speaks Mexican · · · · · · · · · · · · · 103
     7. Festus' Baby Prediction · · · · · · · · · · · · 104
     8. Learn to Read & Write · · · · · · · · · · · · · 105
     9. Deadly Mistaken Identity · · · · · · · · · · · · 105
     10. Rope of Snakes · · · · · · · · · · · · · · · · ·115
     11. Surprise Gunfight in Dodge · · · · · · · · · · ·117

12. A Quiet Day in Dodge	118
13. A Hot Day in Dodge	120
14. It's Scary	122
15. Doc's Pain Pills	123
16. A Cold Draft	123
17. Doc's Escort	124
18. Dr. Newly	125
19. Festus' Ague	125
20. Smokey Hill Country	126
21. Reclaiming Hilt	128
22. Old Nag	128
23. Bad Apples	129
24. Kitty's Orphan Baby	130
25. Festus' Fresh Coffee	131
26. Mule Headedness	132
27. Festus' Posse	133
28. Temporary Marshal	135
29. Doc's Rescue	136
30. Drover Wil	139
31. Family of Outlaws	141
32. Festus' Prisoner	143
33. Ruth Gets Sold	144
34. The Good Samaritan	146
35. Doc's Prized Fishing Pole	148
36. Festus Will Show Up	149
37. Festus & the Preacher	150
38. Silas Killed Ah Dead Man	155
39. Festus' Prisoner, Silas	157

40. Silas Is Not Guilty · · · · · · · · · · · · · · · 159
41. Mathew & Kitty are Gone · · · · · · · · · · 159
42. Matt's Resignation · · · · · · · · · · · · · · · 161
43. Vacation for Matt & Festus · · · · · · · · · 162
44. Where Ya Go'n Mathew? · · · · · · · · · · 163
45. Festus' Gold Piece · · · · · · · · · · · · · · · 165
46. Down & Out Whooly · · · · · · · · · · · · 166
47. Red Paint on a Gold Coin · · · · · · · · · 167
48. 'Money Bags' Festus · · · · · · · · · · · · · 168
49. Good Teamwork · · · · · · · · · · · · · · · · 170
50. Festus Builds the Gallows · · · · · · · · · 171
51. Festus Tears Down the Gallows · · · · · · 172
52. Wonders Never Cease · · · · · · · · · · · · 173
53. Weatherman Festus · · · · · · · · · · · · · 174
54. Doc's Upstanding Patient · · · · · · · · · 175
55. Louie Pheeters is Innocent! · · · · · · · · 177
56. Who Is Thomas Jefferson? · · · · · · · · · 178
57. 100th Meridian · · · · · · · · · · · · · · · · 179
58. Festus' Worstest Best Friend · · · · · · · 181
59. Festus' Patent · · · · · · · · · · · · · · · · · 185
60. Two Quacks in Dodge · · · · · · · · · · · 187
61. The Long Branch Rooster · · · · · · · · · 189
62. Trail Boss Festus · · · · · · · · · · · · · · · 191
63. Everybody Welcome · · · · · · · · · · · · · 192
64. Abelia · 193
65. A Little Peace & Quiet · · · · · · · · · · · 196
66. Doc is Alive & Well · · · · · · · · · · · · · 197
67. Doc's Homecoming · · · · · · · · · · · · · 200

68. Crawdads at Midnight · · · · · · · · · · · · · 202
69. Festus Go'n In'ta Business · · · · · · · · · · 205
70. Festus Crosses the Cimarron · · · · · · · · 206
71. Water Witch'n · · · · · · · · · · · · · · · · · · 208

Post Script · 209

"That men may know wisdom and instruction, understand words of insight, receive instruction in wise dealing, righteousness, justice, and equity; that prudence may be given to the simple, knowledge and discretion to the youth----that a wise man also may hear and increase in learning, and the man of understanding acquire skill, to understand a proverb and a figure, the words of the wise and their riddles."

Proverb 1.1-6
King Solomon
Son of David, King of Israel
Circ. 970-931 BC

Acknowledgement

I WISH TO ACKNOWLEDGE SOUTHERN Methodist University's DeGoyler Library, Manuscript Collection department of Dallas, Texas for the research of selected portions of Gunsmoke episode numbers 626, 636, 614 and 615 scripts from the years 1974-1975. The scripts are from the Milburn Stone collection. The Stone collection of Gunsmoke television scripts are from 1955-1975 episodes. It is comprised of scripts and drafts of episodes of Gunsmoke, the longest running western series on television history.

Foreword

Festus Haggen was best known for his simple 'Hill Country' vocabulary and mannerisms. Although thought to be simple minded by casual observers, Festus had a sharp eye for what was right and wrong in his day to day observations and dealings around Dodge City, Ford County, Kansas. He was not considered by most to be a man of knowledge, because he could neither read nor write, but he possessed considerable native intelligence.

Festus ended up in Dodge City after he assisted Marshal Matt Dillon capture his outlaw uncle, 'Black Jack Haggen'. With no desire to return to 'Haggen Country' he stayed on in Dodge doing odd jobs for folks, and just being a friendly sort to passersby on the street and boardwalk of the town. He managed to get work now and then at the town blacksmith shop, and in exchange for his work he was given a small room and cot in the back of the livery stable where he laid his head at night, and stored his meager belongings that amounted to no more than the clothes on his back, hat on his head, boots on his feet, and a few cooking utensils. His favorite hangouts were the Marshal's office and the Long Branch saloon where he managed to get free beer from people who were taken with his profound tales and stories.

Festus won the trust of U. S. Marshal Matt Dillon, whom he addressed as Mathew, and was made a full time deputy. The job appeared to be his first experience with regular work and an income that amounted to not much more than $4.00 a month, that never seemed to hold him over one month to the next. He was uncanny at getting free beer and meals from his new-found friends.

In one *Gunsmoke*© episode Festus talked about his past life as a trapper and fur trader and his work on the Transcontinental Railroad after the Civil War. He also served in the Confederate States Army and was a staunch defender of General Robert E. Lee's name. According to Festus his mule, Ruth, was named after a mule that was shot and killed by 'Yankees' while carrying Confederate casualties from the battlefield.

He developed a fond and loving relationship with Matt, Kitty Russell, Doc Adams, and Newly O'Brien the town gunsmith and sometime deputy. They are often seen in the Long Branch talking over the days events and events of days past. Although he had numerous cantankerous arguments with Doc, it was all in a days fun trying to get the better of one another.

According to Festus

Ken Curtis as Festus was a constant source of joy, wit and laughter, and he was a gifted entertainer. In his character as Festus he was no saint, but he possessed a deep sense of goodness, loyalty and wisdom. Hence the supporting Biblical Proverbs in **According to Festus** are thought provoking and introspective. They show the humanness of Festus Haggen, and when we look closely into his character we may even see ourselves.

Ruth Ann Hamilton
June 15, 2016

Preface

THE ROLE OF DEPUTY MARSHAL Festus Haggen on the long running western television series, *Gunsmoke©* was played by actor Ken Curtis. He first appeared on the show in 1962 and became full time from 1964 until 1975. Curtis was born Curtis Wayne Gates on July 2, 1916 in Lamar, Prowers County, Colorado to Dan and Nellie (Sneed) Gates. At an early age his parents moved a short distance west to Las Animas, Bent County, Colorado where his father took the job of Bent County sheriff. The family lived on the bottom floor of the jailhouse. The jail cells were on the second floor, and Nellie cooked meals for the prisoners. The jail is now located for historical preservation purposes on the grounds of the Bent County Courthouse in Las Animas.

Ken Curtis was a singer and actor. He performed with the Sons of the Pioneers from 1949 to 1952 and was the lead singer on occasion. Through his first marriage he was the son-in-law of director John Ford. Curtis teamed with Ford and John Wayne in several movies including *Rio Grande, The Searchers, The Alamo,* and *How the West Was Won.* He also appeared on the television series *Death Valley Days.*

Although throughout his career he appeared in over twenty feature films and sixteen television series and specials, Curtis is best remembered for his role as Festus Haggen. He first appeared as Festus in season eight, episode thirteen, *Us Haggens*. His next appearance was with his mule Ruth in *Prairie Wolfer*, season nine episode sixteen. Starring in the role for eleven years, Curtis patterned his character after a man from his childhood by the name of Cedar Jack, who lived several miles outside of town, and who made a living cutting cedar fence posts for ranchers in the area. Festus' character had a twangy nasal tone and rural accent that Curtis developed for the role. His portrayal as Festus ends up being interpreted by viewers as 'lovable' and it kept him on the *Gunsmoke*© series as a full-time cast member.[1]

Ken Curtis as Festus Haggen.[2]

---

[1] Wikipedia.com :Available under the Creative Commons Attribution-Share Alike License. 2016.
[2] Ibid.

Prelude

My parents bought their first television set around 1953. It was a black and white Motorola as I recall. Dad and mom and us kids loved the *Gunsmoke* series from the very first showing in 1955 and never missed an episode if we could help it. We fell in love with the show, the actors and the roles they played. The writers and producers of *Gunsmoke* were quite talented at portraying a sense of 'cattle country' 'instant' justice on the dusty western plains of Kansas and on the streets of Dodge City. United States Marshal Matt Dillon was the central character played by James Arness. Through 1966-75 his primary supporting cast included Doc Adams played by Milburn Stone, Long Branch saloon owner Kitty Russell played by Amanda Blake, and Deputy Marshals Chester Goode played by Dennis Weaver and Festus Haggen played by Ken Cutis, and gunsmith Newly O'Brien played by Buck Taylor.

Six decades and five years have passed since I watched that first *Gunsmoke* episode and today I watch re-runs of it on *TV Land©* telecasts. My opinion of the series has not changed. It was a classic all-time best Western Series! While watching reruns I grew especially fond of the Festus Haggen character and his odd reasoning process, his profound statements, and the way he talked. I have to say he pretty much murdered the King's language, but he got his point across and left little misunderstanding between himself and those he encountered in conversation.

Festus could neither read nor write and it was a continual bone of contention between him and Doc Adams, to the point where Doc went out of his way at every turn to question Festus about his logic or reasoning and his extraordinary statements. They were often seen arguing and ridiculing one another while they stood in the middle of the street of Dodge City, on the boardwalk, in the Marshal's office, or in the Long Branch saloon.

Most often in everyday concerns exchanged between Festus and his friends and others he encountered, including outlaws, there was exposed a profound sense of moral truth and common sense that left them speechless. Often times folks walked away muttering and talking to themselves after a conversation with him. His sayings were not the words of a clever comedian. He was who he was, and he spoke the way he saw life and the way he lived his life with personal responsibility and accountability.

Over a period of several years I made note of some of Festus' comments while watching various episodes. I found it interesting that many of his expressions were common to country folks of my grandfather's generation. Sometime later I decided to gather what I had written and relate them to Biblical truth. **According To Festus** is a collection of 206 selected sayings and 71 paraphrased conversations of wisdom by Festus Haggen that correlate with Biblical Proverbs and Bible[3] references.

In memory of the 100th year of Ken Curtis' birth, I hope you enjoy reading and pondering his words as much as I did when I discerned and compiled them.

Gunsmoke© Main Cast, l-r: Milburn Stone (Doc), Ken Curtis (Festus), Amanda Blake (Kitty), and James Arness (Matt Dillon), cir. 1968.[4]

---

3 The Holy Bible, Old & New Testaments: Revised Standard Version.
4 Wikipedia.com :Available under the Creative Commons Attribution-Share Alike License. 2016.

CHAPTER I

Festus' Sayings[5]

1. "It's as true as wings to a bird!"

Ps. 55.6: And I said, Oh that I had wings like a dove! For then would I fly away, and be at rest.

2. "That feller is slipper'n ah snake through a fence!"

Ps. 58.3-5: The wicked are estranged from the womb; they go astray as soon as they are born, speaking lies. Their poison is like the poison of a serpent; they are like the deaf adder that stoppeth her ear. Which will not hearken to the voice of charmers, charming never so wisely.

---

5 Various sayings of Festus Haggen from Season 12: 1966-67 through Season 20, 1974-75. Wikipedia list of Gunsmoke television episodes. Last modified on 21 May 2016, at 00:59.

3. "Don't ya see?"

Prov. 29.13: The poor man and his oppressor have this in common ~ the Lord gave eyes to both of them.

Prov. 27.12: Sensible people will see trouble coming and avoid it, but an unthinking person will walk right into it and regret it later.

4. "Anyone in God's green earth can do someth'n!"

1Cor. 12.4-6 "There are different kinds of spiritual gifts, but the same Spirit gives them. There are different ways of serving, but the same Lord is served. There are different abilities to perform service, but the same God gives ability to everyone for their particular service."

2Thes. 3.10-11: While we were with you, we used to tell you, "Whoever refuses to work is not allowed to eat." We say this because we hear that there are some people among you who live lazy lives and who do nothing except meddle in other people's business.

5. "The moon and the sun is in the same basket!"

Ps. 19.1-6: How clearly the sky reveals God's glory! How plainly it shows what he has done! Each day announces it to the following day; each night repeats it to the next. No speech or words are used, no sound is heard; yet their voice goes out to all the world and is heard to the ends of the earth. God made a home in the sky for the sun; it comes out in the morning like a happy bridegroom, like an athlete eager to run a race. It starts at one end of the sky and goes across to the other. Nothing can hide from its heat.

Gen. 1.16-18: So God made the two larger lights, the sun to rule over the day and the moon to rule over the night; he also made the stars. He placed the lights in the sky to shine on the earth, to rule over the day and the night, and to separate light from darkness. And God was pleased with what he saw.

Ps. 8.3-4: When I look at thy heavens, the work of thy fingers, the moon and the stars which thou hast established; what is man that thou art mindful of him, and the son of man that thou dost care for him?

6. "He fights like a burnt bear and ah nest full of hornets!"

Deut. 1.44: Then the Amorites who lived in those hills came out against you like a swarm of bees. They chased you as far as Hormah and defeated you there in the hill country of Edom.

7. "What I'm ah say'n ain't go'n through yer head!"

Prov. 12.15: Stupid people always think they are right. Wise people listen to advice.

8. "Those two hay-heads been argu'n twixt themselves!"

Prov. 29.9: When an intelligent man brings a lawsuit against a fool, the fool only laughs and becomes loud and abusive.

Prov. 25.9: If you and your neighbor have a difference of opinion, settle it between yourselves and do not reveal any secrets.

9. "If ya git a slipperty man ya can't shake, make him ah neighbor so ya can keep an eye on him!"

Prov. 12.20: Those who plan evil are in for a rude surprise, but those who work for good will find happiness.

Prov. 26.18-20: A man who tricks someone and then claims that he is only joking is like a crazy man playing with a deadly weapon. Without wood, a fire goes out; without gossip, quarreling stops.

Ps. 35.4-6: May those who try to kill me be defeated and disgraced! May those who plot against me be turned back and confused! May they be like straw blown by the wind. May their path be dark and slippery while the angel of the Lord strikes them down.

10. "I've never felt so hog tied in all my life!"

Ps. 88.15: Ever since I was young, I have suffered and been near death; I am worn out from the burden of your punishments.

Jer. 6.21-24: And So I will make these people stumble and fall. Fathers and sons will die and so will friends and neighbors. The Lord says, "People are coming from a country in the north; a mighty nation far away is preparing for war. They have taken up their bows and swords; they are cruel and merciless. They sound like the roaring sea, as they ride their horses. They are ready for battle against Jerusalem." "We have heard the news," say the people of Jerusalem, "and our hands hang limp; we are seized by anguish and pain like a woman in labor."

11. "Let's stop here fer the night and move on at first light!"

Prov. 4.18: The road the righteous travel is like the sunrise, getting brighter and brighter until daylight has come.

Ps. 97.11: Light shines on the righteous
and gladness on the good.

12. "My right hand had a bet with my left in that tussle I had with that feller!"

Prov. 16.32-33: It is better to be patient than powerful. It is better to win control over yourself than over whole cities. Men cast lots to learn God's will, but God himself determines the answer.

Prov. 25.9: If you and your neighbor have a difference of opinion, settle it between yourselves and do not reveal any secrets.

13. "You got a head like a cantaloupe, don't ya see?"

Prov. 16.22: Wisdom is a fountain of life to the wise, but trying to educate stupid people is a waste of time.

Prov. 18.7: When a fool speaks, he is ruining himself; he gets caught in the trap of his own words.

Prov. 10.8: Sensible people accept good advice. People who talk foolishly will come to ruin.

14. "Yer talk'n like my foot's asleep!"[6]

Prov. 26.28: You have to hate someone to want to hurt him with lies. Insincere talk brings nothing but ruin.

Prov. 4.24: Put away from you crooked speech, and put devious talk far from you.

---

6 1966-67: Season 12, Series No. 428, No. 19 in season, written by Calvin Clements, Sr.

15. "Could I buy you fellers a drink," Asks Doc, and Festus says, "Does a mule have ears?"

Prov. 31.7: Let them drink and forget their poverty, and remember their misery no more.

16. "That's very thoughtfulness of ya Kitty!"

Prov. 12.5: The thoughts of the righteous are just; the counsels of the wicked are treacherous.

Prov. 1.23: Give heed to my reproof; behold, I will pour out my thoughts to you; I will make my words known to you.

17. "That's the only'est time I ever did see such ah thing happen like that!"

Is. 5.20: Woe to those who call evil good and good evil, who put darkness for light and light for darkness, who put bitter for sweet and sweet for bitter!

18. "The sun don't shine on a dog's rear-end every day!"

Prov. 26.1: Like snow in summer or rain in harvest, so honor is not fitting for a fool.

Ecc. 9.11-12: Again, I saw that under the sun the race is not to the swift, nor the battle to the strong, nor bread to the wise, nor riches to the intelligent, nor favor to the men of skill; but time and chance happen to them all. For man does not know his time. Like fish that are taken in an evil net, and like birds that are caught in a snare, so the sons of men are snared at an evil time, when it suddenly falls upon them.

Matt. 5.44-45: "But I say to you, Love your enemies and pray for those who persecute you, so that you may be sons of your Father who is in heaven; for He makes His sun rise on the evil and on the good, and sends rain on the just and on the unjust."

19. "She could talk a hind leg off ah mule!"

Prov. 14.3: The talk of a fool is a rod for his back, but the lips of the wise will preserve them.

Prov. 20.19: He who goes about gossiping reveals secrets; therefore do not associate with one who speaks foolishly.

1Tim. 5.13: Besides that, they learn to be idlers, gadding about from house to house, and not only idlers but gossips and busybodies, saying what they should not.

20. "She prattles on like rain on the roof!"

Prov. 16.27-28: A worthless man plots evil, and his speech is like a scorching fire. A perverse man spreads strife, and a whisperer separates close friends.

Prov. 30.32: If you have been foolish, exalting yourself, or if you have been devising evil, put your hand on your mouth.

Prov. 9.13: A foolish woman is noisy; she is wanton and knows no shame.

Prov. 31.10, 26: A good wife who can find? She is far more precious than jewels. She opens her mouth with wisdom, and the teaching of kindness is on her tongue.

21. "Well, if that don't peel the skin off ah snake!"

Jer. 13.23: Can the Ethiopian change his skin or the leopard his spots? Then also you can do good who are accustomed to do evil.

22. "I'll git on ya like stink on ah skunk!"

Prov. 15.10: There is severe discipline for him who forsakes the way; he who hates reproof will die.

23. "Anything happens ta Mathew I'll get on ya like thunder after light'n, an I'll take ah oath on that!"[6.1]

24. "If I catch ya poly-fox'n around here, I'll be on ya like ugly on ah ape!"[6.2]

Prov. 17.10: A rebuke goes deeper into a man of understanding than a hundred blows into a fool.

6.1 1967-68: Season 13, Series No. 440, No. 2 in season, written by Clyde Ware.
6.2 1967-68: Season 13, Series No. 458, No. 20 in season, written by Calvin Clements, Sr.

Prov. 24.24-25: He who says to the wicked, 'You are innocent,' will be cursed by peoples, abhorred by nations; but those who rebuke the wicked will have delight, and a good blessing will be upon them.

25. "That old wagon on this here road bounced and shook my entire born-put-together!"

Ecc. 1.8: All things are full of weariness; a man cannot utter it; the eye is not satisfied with seeing, nor the ear filled with hearing.

Ecc. 12.11-12: The sayings of the wise are like goads, and like nails firmly fixed are the collected sayings that are given by one Shepherd. My son, beware of anything beyond these. Of making many books there is no end, and much study is a weariness of the flesh.

26. "I've seen greed in a hog's eye before and I'm see'n it in yours!"

Prov. 11.24,26: One man gives freely, yet grows all the richer; another withholds what he should give, and only suffers want. The people curse him who holds back grain, but a blessing is on the head of him who sells it.

Jer. 6.13: "For from the least to the greatest of them, every one is greedy for unjust gain; and from prophet to priest, everyone deals falsely."

Prov. 30.15: The leech has two daughters; "Give, give," they cry. Three things are never satisfied; four never say, "Enough."

---

27. "The more things a fellers got on his mind, the more it's harder to think of more than one thing! Don't ya see?"

Prov. 14.30: A tranquil mind gives life to the flesh, but passion makes the bones rot.

Prov.16.9: A man's mind plans his way, but the Lord directs his steps.

Prov. 27.19: As in water, face answers to face, so the mind of man reflects the man.

---

28. "Young'ns today ain't got enough ambition to pour sand down a rat hole!"[6.3]

6.3 1967-68: Season 13, Series No. 456, No. 18 in season, written by Robert Totten.

Prov.12.24: The hand of the diligent will rule, while the slothful will be put to forced labor.

Prov. 13.4: The soul of the sluggard craves, and gets nothing, while the soul of the diligent is richly supplied.

⸺⸻

29. "Mathew will tell ya what you can do with yer Cattleman's 'Copperative'!"[7]

Prov. 4.14, 16: Do not enter the path of the wicked, and do not walk in the way of evil men. For they cannot sleep unless they have done wrong; they are robbed of sleep unless they have made some one stumble.

⸺⸻

30. "See those skilky strangers a hang'n around the bank? A rat potates jist like em!"

Prov. 3.31-32: Do not envy a man of violence and do not choose any of his ways; for the perverse man is an abomination to the Lord, but the upright are in his confidence.

⸺⸻

---

[7] 1967-68: Season 13, Series No. 455, No. 17 in season, written by Calvin Clements, Jr.

According to Festus

31. "How would ya like to be gather'n eggs an find HER on the nest?"[7.1]

Prov. 31.30: Charm is deceitful, and beauty is vain, but a woman who fears the Lord is to be praised.

Prov. 6.8: She prepares her food in summer, and gathers her sustenance in harvest.

32. "All day they've had me hop'n around like ah flea on a hot skillet!"[7.2]

Prov. 6.27-28: Can a man carry fire in his bosom and his clothes not be burned? Or can one walk upon hot coals and his feet not be scorched?

33. "Now don't fret Mathew, everything is go'n to be as right as rain!"

Job 5.8-11: "As for me, I would seek God, and to God would I commit my cause; who does great things and unsearchable, marvelous things without

---

[7.1] 1967-68: Season 13, Series No. 458, No. 20 in season, written by Calvin Clements, Sr.
[7.2] Ibid.

number: he gives rain upon the earth and sends waters upon the fields; he sets on high those who are lowly, and those who mourn are lifted to safety."

---

34. "I could have saved ya a whole piece of miserables and suffer'n!"[7.3]

Prov. 14.8: The wisdom of a prudent man is to discern his way, but the folly of fools is deceiving.

---

35. "I feel like a near-sighted ninny. I ain't broke no trail on that feller anywhere in these parts and I been turn'n over every rock!"[7.4]

Prov. 1.27-28: When panic strikes you like a storm, and your calamity comes like a whirlwind, when distress and anguish come upon you. Then they will call upon me, but I will not answer; they will seek me diligently but will not find me.

[7.3] 1967-68: Season 13, Series No. 460, No. 22 in season, written by Calvin Clements, Jr.
[7.4] 1967-68: Season 13, Series No. 461, No. 23 in season, written by Calvin Clements, Sr.

36. Festus says to Doc, "Why don't ya jist go roll yourself a pill?"[7.5]

Prov. 10.17: He who heeds instruction is on the path to life, but he who rejects reproof goes astray.

Prov. 14.29: He who is slow to anger has great understanding, but he who has a hasty temper exalts folly.

37. "You couldn't bust a bird's egg with a ball-peen hammer!"[7.6]

Prov. 1.17-19: For in vain is a net spread in the sight of any bird; but these men lie in wait for their own blood, they set an ambush for their own lives. Such are the ways of all who get gain by violence; it takes away the life of its possessors.

Ps. 124.6-7: Blessed be the Lord, who has not given us as prey to their teeth! We have escaped as a bird from the snare of the fowlers; the snare is broken, and we have escaped!

7.5 Ibid.
7.6 Ibid. 7.6 1967-68: Season 13, Series No. 463, No. 25 in season, written by Anthony Ellis.

38. Doc tells Festus, "You can catch more flies with honey!" And Festus says, "Who wants a mess of flies stuck in honey?"[7.7]

Ecc. 10.1: Dead flies make the perfumer's ointment give off an evil odor; so a little folly outweighs wisdom and honor.[7.8]

Ex. 8.21: Else, if you will not let my people go, behold, I will send swarms of flies on you and your servants and your people, and into your houses; and the houses of the Egyptians shall be filled with swarms of flies, and also the ground on which they stand.

---

39. "That ole nag doesn't look like he's got six ticks left in him!"

Ecc. 3.1-2: For everything there is a season, and a time for every matter under heaven: a time to be born and a time to die;

Ecc. 8.6: For every matter has its time and way, although man's trouble lies heavy upon him.

[7.7] 1968-69: Season 14, Series No. 467, No. 4 in season, written by Calvin Clements, Sr.
[7.8] 1968-69: Season 14, Series No. 471, No. 8 in season, written by Calvin Clements, Sr.

40. "Ya haven't got the courage of a moth banging on ah winder!"

Ps. 27.14: Wait for the Lord; be strong, and let your heart take courage; yea, wait for the Lord!

Ezek. 22.14: "Can your courage endure, or can your hands be strong, in the days that I shall deal with you? I the Lord have spoken, and I will do it."

―❦―

41. "That store-man orta be wear'n ah mask asking ah price like that!"

Prov. 20.10: Diverse weights and diverse measures are both alike an abomination to the Lord.

―❦―

42. "Golly-gee-gum and beat a pole cat in a bear holler!"

Prov. 10.26: Like vinegar to the teeth, and smoke to the eyes, so is the sluggard to those who send him.

―❦―

43. "Now see here young'ns, ya be as quiet as ah cotton-tail on green grass!"

Ecc. 4.6: Better is a handful of quietness than two hands full of toil and a striving after the wind.

44. "Ya shut your tater trap too!"

Prov. 4.24: Put away from you crooked speech, and put devious talk far from you.

45. "It sure was pleasurable meet'n up with ya. I sure wish I could have met ya under more pleasurable circumstances maam."[8]

Ecc. 2.10: And whatever my eyes desired I did not keep from them; I kept my heart from no pleasure, for my heart found pleasure in all my toil, and this was the reward for all my toil.

---

8 1968-69: Season 14, Series No. 471, No. 8 in season, written by Calvin Clements, Sr.

46. "It makes ya feel plum soulsome don't it Mathew?"[8.1]

Prov. 2.10: For wisdom will come into your heart, and knowledge will be pleasant to your soul.

Prov. 3.17-18: Her ways are ways of pleasantness, and all her paths are peace. She is a tree of life to those who lay hold of her; those who hold her fast are called happy.

Ps. 133.1: Behold, How good and pleasant it is when brothers dwell in unity.

47. "Drop that knife before I carve ya up from yer belly to yer back-bone! Now git out of Dodge!"

Prov. 28.1: The wicked flee when no one pursues, but the righteous are bold as a lion.

48. "I got ah bad disposition, 'cause I was raised on sour milk!"

Job 10.1,10: "I loathe my life; I will give free utterance to my complaint; I will speak in the

---

[8.1] 1967-68: Season 13, Series No. 441 No. 3in season, written by Calvin Clements, Sr.

bitterness of my soul. Didst thou not pour me out like milk and curdle me like cheese?"

—⁂—

49. "It's ah free country, but it's git'n to cost more and more everyday!"

Lk. 14.28: "For which of you, desiring to build a tower, does not first sit down and count the cost, whether he has enough to complete it?"

Gal. 5.13: For you were called to freedom, brethren, only do not use your freedom as an opportunity for the flesh, but through love, be servants of one another.

—⁂—

50. "Let's ride together like old times Mathew, so lets git started!"

Prov. 17.17: A friend loves at all times, and a brother is born for adversity.

Prov. 19.6: Many seek the favor of a generous man, and every one is a friend to a man who gives gifts.

Prov. 27.6: Faithful are the wounds of a friend; profuse are the kisses of an enemy.

Jn. 15.13: "Greater love has no man than this, that a man lay down his life for his friends."

⸻

51. Matt says to Festus, "I've seen you track a snake across pine needles."

Job 19.22: "Why do you, like God, pursue me? Why are you not satisfied with my flesh?"

Ps. 83.13, 15: O my God, make them like whirling dust, like chaff before the wind. So do thou pursue them with thy tempest and terrify them with thy hurricane.

Lam. 3.66: "Thou wilt pursue them in anger and destroy them from under thy heavens, O Lord."

⸻

52. "He got away 'cause he's smoother'n hair on a frog!"

Ps. 124.7: We have escaped as a bird from the snare of the fowlers; the snare is broken, and we have escaped!

⸻

53. "Ain't that a tear-some thing!"

Ps. 42.3: My tears have been my food day and night, while men say to me continually, "Where is your God?"

Ps. 56.8: Thou hast kept count of my tossings; put thou my tears in thy bottle! Are they not in thy Book?

―⸺

54. "He's ah fast draw, and if"n ya were to take a snake's tongue and grease it and tie it to ah light'n bolt, ya couldn't git anything faster'n that, and that's ah fact. I'll guarantee ya!"[8.2]

Prov. 10.31: The mouth of the righteous brings forth wisdom, but the perverse tongue will be cut off.

Ps. 18.14: And he sent out his arrows, and scattered them; he flashed forth lightnings, and routed them.

Ps. 35.6: Let the way be dark and slippery, with the angel of the Lord pursuing them!

―⸺

[8.2] 1968-69: Season 14, Series No. 481, No. 18 in season, written by Calvin Clements, Sr.

55. "He's grin'n like ah cat eat'n cactus."[8.3]

Prov. 18.7: A fool's mouth is his ruin, and
his lips are a snare to himself.

Ecc. 2.23: For all his days are full of pain, and
his work is a vexation; even in the night his
mind does not rest. This also is vanity.

---

56. Festus says to Newly, "Ya ain't the first one to sweep ah girl off''n her feet, after all she said ya were all powerful!"[9]

Prov. 4.6: Do not forsake her, and she will keep
you; love her, and she will guard you.

Prov. 8.17: I love those who love me, and
those who seek me diligently find me.

8.3 1968-69: Season 14, Series No. 481, No. 18 in season, written by Calvin Clements, Sr.
9 1968-69: Season 14, Series No. 481, No. 18 in season, written by Calvin Clements, Sr.

57. "With all that school'n he's still dumber than ah stick!"

Prov. 1.8-9: Hear my son, your father's instruction, and reject not your mother's teaching; for they are a fair garland for your head, and pendants for your neck.

Prov. 13.14: The teaching of the wise is a fountain of life, that one may avoid the snares of death.

―⸺

58. "He'll catch fire quicker'n last years haystack, I'll guarantee ya that!"[9.1]

Ps. 39.2-3: I was dumb and silent, I held my peace to no avail; my distress grew worse, my heart became hot within me. As I mused, the fire burned; then I spoke with my tongue.

―⸺

59. "This whole gold dig'n thing is crooked'ner ah dog's hind leg!"

Prov. 26.18-19: Like a madman who throws firebrands, arrows, and death, is the man who deceives his neighbor and says, "I am only joking!"

9.1 1967-68: Season 13, Series No. 440, No. 2 in season, written by Clyde Ware.

Ecc. 12.14: For God will bring every deed into judgment, with every secret thing, whether good or evil.

Job 12.16: "With him are strength and wisdom; the deceived and the deceiver are his."

⸻

60. Doc says to Festus, "If you put your brains in a mustard seed, they would rattle around like a peanut in a boxcar!"

Prov. 8.5: O simple ones, learn prudence; O foolish men, pay attention.

Matt. 13.31-32: "The kingdom of heaven is like a grain of mustard seed which a man took and sowed in his field; it is the smallest of all seeds, but when it has grown it is the greatest of shrubs and becomes a tree, so that the birds of the air come and make nests in its branches."

⸻

61. "Yer git'n short on politedness and long on cussedness!"

Prov. 29.15: The rod and reproof give wisdom, but a child left to him self brings shame to his mother.

Ecc. 10.20: Even in your thought, do not curse the king, nor in your bedchamber curse the rich; for a bird of the air will carry your voice, or some winged creature, tell the matter.

―⸺

62. "If anything happens to this feller whilst I'm gone, I'll peel the hide off yer carcass!"

Ps. 41.3, 9: The Lord sustains him on his sickbed; in his illness thou healest all his infirmities. Even my bosom friend in whom I trusted, who ate of my bread, has lifted his heel against me.

―⸺

63. "He don't want to know the truth even if his head is turned on backwards!"

Prov. 12.17: He who speaks the truth gives honest evidence, but a false witness utters deceit.

Prov. 23.23: Buy truth and do not sell it; buy wisdom, instruction, and understanding.

―⸺

64. "Here's mud in yer eyeball!"

Rom. 13.7: Pay all of them their dues, taxes to whom taxes are due, revenue to whom revenue is due, respect to whom respect is due, honor to whom honor is due.

---

65. Doc tells Festus, "You know this day was starting off just fine, and I'm going to keep it that way!"

Ps. 133.1: Behold, how good and pleasant it is when brothers dwell in unity!

---

66. "You two mutton-heads make me sick!"

Ps. 38.13: But I am like a deaf man, I do not hear, like a dumb man who does not open his mouth. Yea, I am like a man who does not hear, and in whose mouth are no rebukes.

Ps. 39.2: I was dumb and silent, I held my peace to no avail; my distress grew worse;

67. "I don't care about no 'teletygraph' when I'm ah constentrat'n on play'n checkers!"

Jer. 12.5: If you have raced with men on foot, and they have wearied you, how will you compete with horses? And if in a safe land you fall down, how will you do in the jungle of the Jordan?

1Cor. 9.24: Do you not know that in a race all the runners compete, but only one receives the prize? So run that you may obtain it.

68. "That ole pile of rocks called ah farm hasn't had ah blade of grass on it since the upheaval of creation!"

Ps. 37.1-2: Fret not yourself because of the wicked, be not envious of the wrongdoers! For they will soon fade like the grass, and whither like the green herb.

Ps. 103.15-16: As for man, his days are like grass; he flourishes like a flower of the field; for the wind passes over it, and it is gone, and its place knows it no more.

Is. 5.24: Therefore, as the tongue of fire devours the stubble, and as dry grass sinks down in the flame, so their root will be as rottenness, and their blossom go up like dust, for they have rejected the law of the Lord of hosts, and have despised the Word of the Holy One of Israel.

---

69. "Did ya ever wonder how underintakers come by their names; such as the likes of ole Percy Crump in Dodge, ole Moss Feester over in Hays, and ole Feece Moster in Spiritville?"

Prov. 22.1: A good name is to be chosen rather than great riches, and favor is better than silver or gold.

Ecc. 7.1: A good name is better than precious ointment; and the day of death, than the day of birth.

---

70. Doc asked Matt to go fishing with him as Festus approaches them on the boardwalk. "Don't say nothing about Festus going with us." "About what," asks Festus. "Going fishing," says Doc. "Pfffft who says I want to go fish'n with you, but whose go'n to dig yer worms for ya and clean yer fish Doc?"[9.1]

9.1 Various sayings of Festus Haggen from Season 12, 1966-67 through Season 20, 1974-75. Wikipedia list of Gunsmoke television episodes. Last modified on 21 May 2016, at 00:59.

71. "Now lookie here Doc, ya got'a git someth'n shimmery and shiny fer that fish to go-at when yer ah fish'n!"

>Prov. 18.19: A brother helped is like a strong city,
>but quarreling is like the bars of a castle.

72. "You seem to have something weighing heavy on your mind, what is it Festus," Doc asks. "Well I jist don't know," Festus says. "Well then tell us what you do know and it won't take so long," says Doc.[9.2]

>Prov. 14.30: A tranquil mind gives life to the
>flesh, but passion makes the bones rot.

>Prov. 16.9: A man's mind plans his way,
>but the Lord directs his steps.

>Prov. 28.26: He who trusts in his own mind is a fool;
>but he who walks in wisdom will be delivered.

[9.2] Ibid.

73. "Everything's fine as frog hair here Matthew!"

Prov. 4.23: Keep your heart with all vigilance;
for from it flow the springs of life.

---

74. "That don't make no thimble full of sense!"

---

75. "Ruth here is got more sense than all ah them yahoos put tagether, an that's ah fact!"[9.3]

Prov. 21.30: No wisdom, no understanding,
no counsel, can avail against the Lord.

---

76. "If ya don't beat all, that's no more sense than pound'n sand down ah rat hole!"

Prov. 1.20-21: Wisdom cries aloud in the street; in the markets she raises her voice; on the top of the walls she cries out; at the entrance of the city gates she speaks;

9.3   1967-68: Season 13, Series No. 444, No. 6 in season, written by Ron Bishop.

77. "You're like ah side-winder in the hand of ah cottontail!"

Mk. 16.17-18: "And these signs will accompany those who believe: in my name they will cast out demons; they will speak in new tongues; they will pick up serpents, and if they drink any deadly thing, it will not hurt them; they will lay their hands on the sick, and they will recover."

78. "I ain't gunna stuff any of that stuff in my gullet!"

Lam. 4.4-5: "The tongue of the nursling cleaves to the roof of its mouth for thirst; the children beg for food, but no one gives to them. Those who feasted on dainties perish in the streets; those who were brought up in purple lie on ash heaps."

79. "If it hadn't been for these here euchres you'd got along jist fine, and that's ah o'lee fact!"

Prov. 4.14-16: Do not enter the path of the wicked, and do not walk in the way of evil men. Avoid it; do not go on it, turn away from it and pass on. For they cannot sleep unless they have done wrong; they are robbed of sleep unless they have made some one stumble.

Prov. 6.16-19: There are six things which the Lord hates, seven which are an abomination to him: haughty eyes, a lying tongue, and hands that shed innocent blood, a heart that devises wicked plans, feet that make haste to run to evil, a false witness who breathes out lies, and a man who sows discord among brothers.

---

80. Stop banging your ear like that, it makes me nervous," Doc tells Festus. "I don't care if it's ah make'n ya nervyous, it makes it better fer me, don't ya see," says Festus.[9.4]

Prov. 12.25: Anxiety in a man's heart weighs him down, but a good word makes him glad.

Ps. 142.4: I look to the right and watch, but there is none who takes notice of me; no refuge remains to me, no man cares for me.

---

81. "When I been real thirsty, I have lapped dirty water from ah hoof print and been darn glad of it!"

Prov. 25.23: The north wind brings forth rain; and a backbiting tongue, angry looks.

9.4 Various sayings of Festus Haggen from Season 12, 1966-67 through Season 20, 1974-75. Wikipedia list of Gunsmoke television episodes. Last modified on 21 May 2016, at 00:59.

Ps. 107.4: Some wandered in desert wastes,
finding no way to a city to dwell in; hungry and
thirsty, their soul fainted within them.

Matt. 25.35: For I was hungry and you gave
me food, I was thirsty and you gave me drink,
I was a stranger and you welcomed me,

―∽―

82. "Mathew, Have you noticed how pecuriate'n Newly is act'n lately? Why you can't hardly turn around an there's a she-male hanging around on his arm!" Matt says, "Well Festus what's the matter with that, he's single isn't he?" "Well so am I," Festus says.[10]

Prov. 31.30: Charm is deceitful, and beauty is vain,
but a woman who fears the Lord is to be praised.

Prov. 4.6: Do not forsake her, and she will keep
you; love her, and she will guard you.

Prov. 6.25-26: Do not desire her beauty in your
heart, and do not let her capture you with her
eyelashes; for a harlot may be hired for a loaf of
bread, but an adulteress stalks a man's very life.

---

10 971-72: Season 17, Series No. 557, No. 18 in season, written by Wm. Kelley.

Prov. 8.17: I love those who love me, and those who seek me diligently find me.

⤴

93. "I saw these fellers before cause they had ah little bailiwick out side of town like they was ah wait'n fer somebody!"

Prov. 30.14: There are those whose teeth are swords, whose teeth are knives, to devour the poor from off the earth, the needy from among men.

Ps. 7.14-15: Behold, the wicked man conceives evil, and is pregnant with mischief, and brings forth lies, He makes a pit, digging it out, and falls into the hole which he has made.

⤴

94. "I smell trouble and I'll bet you my life's months pay that feller ain't hang'n round here jist to play the pyana!"[11]

Prov. 27.9: Oil and perfume make the heart glad, but the soul is torn by trouble.

---

11 1969-70: Season 15, Series No. 501, No. 12 in season, written by Kay Lenard & Jess Carneol.

Job 3.26: "I am not at ease, nor am I quiet; I have no rest; but trouble comes."

―⸻

95. "I'm go'n to marry her right off soon," Festus' long lost sluggardly friend, Purdy Krepps says. "So what makes ya think in ah mules-eye that she would want ta marry you," asks Festus.[11.1]

Prov. 21.25: The desire of the sluggard kills him for his hands refuse to labor.

Heb. 13.4: Let marriage be held in honor among all, and let the marriage bed be undefiled; for God will judge the immoral and adulterous.

―⸻

96. "And that's ah pure o'lee fact!"

Prov. 12.17: He who speaks the truth gives honest evidence, but a false witness utters deceit.

Prov. 12.19: Truthful lips endure forever, but a lying tongue is but for a moment.

11.1 Various sayings of Festus Haggen from Season 12, 1966-67 through Season 20, 1974-75. Wikipedia list of Gunsmoke television episodes. Last modified on 21 May 2016, at 00:59.

> Prov. 14.25: A truthful witness saves lives,
> but one who utters lies is a betrayer.

----

97. "The wind was blow'n dust so thick ya couldn't stir it with ah stick!"

> Ps. 55.8: I would haste to find me a shelter
> from the raging wind and tempest.

> Ecc. 3.20: All go to one place; all are from
> the dust, and all turn to dust again.

> Ecc. 12.7: And the dust returns to the earth as it
> was, and the Spirit returns to God who gave it.

> Jn. 3.8: The wind blows where it wills, and you hear the
> sound of it, but you do not know whence it comes or whither
> it goes, so it is with everyone who is born of the Spirit."

----

98. Festus walks into the Long Branch and sees Doc at the bar with Kitty and is calculating on getting a free drink and he starts clearing his throat: "I can't git rid of this hackety cough. It must be all that prairity dust

blow'n about Dodge all day!" Doc says, "Kitty don't do it! He's after a free drink again!"[11.2]

Prov. 25.21: If your enemy is hungry, give him bread to eat; and if he is thirsty, give him water to drink;

Prov. 5.15: Drink water from your own cistern, flowing water from your own well.

---

99. "Drop it! Or I'll part yer hair!"

Prov. 13.10: By insolence the heedless make strife, but with those who take advice is wisdom.

Prov. 17.19: He who loves transgression loves strife; He who makes his door high seeks destruction.

Ps. 68.18: Thou didst ascend the high mount, leading captives in thy train, and receiving gifts among men, even among the rebellious, that the Lord God may dwell there.

11.2 Ibid.

100. "Ya come ta Dodge ah boy, but ya sure ain't leav'n one! Adyoose!"[12]

Eph. 4.14: So that we may no longer be children tossed to and fro and carried about with every wind of doctrine, by the cunning of men by their craftiness in deceitful wiles.

1Cor. 2.6: Yet among the mature we do impart wisdom, although it is not a wisdom of this age or of the rulers of this age, who are doomed to pass away.

1Cor. 13.11: When I was a child I spoke like a child, I thought like a child, I reasoned like a child; when I became a man, I gave up childish ways.

Prov. 22.6: Train up a child in the way he should go, and when he is old he will not depart from it.

Prov. 20.11: Even a child makes himself known by his acts, whether what he does is pure and right.

101. "This here coffee is stronger'n ah billy goat's breath!"

Prov. 31.6-7: Give strong drink to him who is perishing, and wine to those in bitter distress; Let them drink and forget their poverty, and remember their misery no more.

---

12 1966-67: Season 12, Series No. 428, No. 19 in season, written by Calvin Clements, Sr.

Ecc. 3.19: For the fate of the sons of men and the fate of beasts is the same; as one dies, so dies the other. They all have the same breath, and man has no advantage over the beasts; for all is vanity.

102. "Ole Doc Adams says ya doctors have some kind of hipocritical someth'n or other don't ya see," Festus tells a new doctor in Dodge.[13]

Zech. 8.17: "Do not devise evil in your hearts against one another, and love no false oath, for all these things I hate, says the Lord."

1Cor. 12.9: To another faith by the same Spirit, to another gifts of healing by the one Spirit.

103. "Don't be ah go'n shoot'n all the dogs jist 'cause one of 'em has fleas!"

Prov. 29.14: If a king judges the poor with equity, his throne will be established forever.

---

13 1971-72: Season 17, Series No. 544, No. 5 in season, written by Jack Miller.

Ps. 75.2: At the set time that I appoint I will judge with equity.

―⁂―

104. "Jist as sure as big steers an summer light'n, things is go'n ta be different around here, I'll guarantee it!"

Ps. 102.25-27: Of old thou didst lay the foundation of the earth, and the heavens are the work of thy hands. They will perish, but thou dost endure: they will all wear out like a garment. Thou changest them like raiment, and they pass away; but thou art the same, and thy years have no end.

―⁂―

105. "Ya mean ta tell me, ya know this tangle footed yahoo here?"

Prov. 19.4: Wealth brings many new friends,
but a poor man is deserted by his friend.

Prov. 19.6-8: Many seek the favor of a generous man, and every one is a friend to a man who gives gifts. All a poor man's brothers hate him; how much more do his friends go far from him! He pursues them with words, but does not have them.

―⁂―

106. "Ya draw those bad critters to ya like ants ta garbage!"

Prov. 16.28-30: A perverse man spreads strife, and a whisperer separates close friends. A man of violence entices his neighbor and leads him in a way that is not good. He who winks his eyes plans perverse things, he who compresses his lips brings evil to pass.

―⸺

107. "Ya've got about as much life in ya as a toad in a snow-storm!"

Prov. 6.6-8: Go to the ant, O sluggard; consider her ways, and be wise. Without having any chief officer or ruler, she prepares her food in summer, and gathers her sustenance in harvest.

Prov. 13.4: The soul of the sluggard craves, and gets nothing, while the soul of the diligent is richly supplied.

―⸺

108. "I'm broker an flatter than ah snake through a ringer!"

Prov. 10.15: A rich man's wealth is his strong city; the poverty of the poor is their ruin.

Ecc. 5.10-11: He who loves money will not be satisfied with money; nor he who loves wealth, with gain: this also is vanity. When the goods increase; they increase who eat them; and what gain has their owner but to see them with his eyes?

⁓⸺

109. "Like us Haggens always say, ah feller can't choose his neighbors or his relations, but he sure can choose his friends!"

Prov. 18.24: There are friends who pretend to be friends, but there is a friend who sticks closer than a brother.

⁓⸺

110. Festus confronts a snake-oil salesman and self-professed healer in Dodge City: "Now see here mister, we got ah 'ornadance' in this here town that says that ya can't sell no portions of no kind, how so everly without ole Doc Adams ah proof'n on it first before that it's fit'n fer public 'conumption'!"[14]

Prov. 26.18-19: Like a madman who throws firebrands, arrows, and death, is the man who deceives his neighbor and says, "I am only joking!"

---

14 1969-70: Season 15, Series No. 507, No. 18 in season, written by Benny Rubin.

Prov. 26.23: Like the glaze covering an earthen
vessel are smooth lips with an evil heart.

---

111. "That ole scudder Doc, he's ah work'n like ah coal miner's mule!"

Prov. 12.14: From the fruit of his words a man is satisfied with
good, and the work of a man's hand comes back to him.

Prov. 16.3: Commit your work to the Lord,
and your plans will be established.

Prov. 31.10,13: A good wife who can find? She
is far more precious than jewels. She seeks wool
and flax, and works with willing hands.

---

112. "Now see here Doc, they ain't no use'n ya git'n all humped up like ah mad ant!"

Prov. 14.29: He who is slow to anger has great
understanding, but he who has a hasty temper exalts folly.

Prov. 15.18: A hot-tempered man stirs up strife, but
he who is slow to anger quiets contention.

Prov. 16.32: He who is slow to anger is better than the mighty, and he who rules his spirit than he who takes a city.

---

113. "Well who are you anyway," a stranger asks Festus. "My name is Festus Haggen if'n it's any of yer look-out!"[15]

Prov. 22.1: A good name is to be chosen rather than great riches, and favor is better than silver or gold.

Ecc. 7.1: A good name is better than precious ointment; and the day of death, than the day of birth.

---

114. "Mathew, I've eyeballed that whole shebang down there at that shack an could be I could shake 'em out by my ownself whilst ya circle back around ta the other side. Don't ya see? So lets git at er!"[15.1]

Ps. 83.14-15: As fire consumes the forest, as the flame sets the mountains ablaze, so do thou pursue them with thy tempest and terrify them with thy hurricane.

---

15 1974-75: Season 20, Series No. 614, No. 3 in season, written by Paul Savage.
15.1 Various sayings of Festus Haggen from Season 12, 1966-67 through Season 20, 1974-75. Wikipedia list of Gunsmoke television episodes. Last modified on 21 May 2016, at 00:59.

115. Festus took a bad blow to the head in a gunfight when he saved Doc's life and Doc has him on his examination table and says: "Festus, can you see me?" "I'm all swirmiated. I can't see ya too well Doc, but I'm a'see'n that yer git'n uglier everyday!"[16]

Prov. 17.10: A rebuke goes deeper into a man of understanding than a hundred blows into a fool.

Jn. 15.13: "Greater love has no man than this, that a man lay down his life for his friends."

⸺⁶

116. "Ah few more days like this an my tail will take root in my saddle!"

Ecc. 1.8: All things are full of weariness; a man cannot utter it; the eye is not satisfied with seeing, nor the ear filled with hearing.

Ecc. 10.15: The toil of a fool wearies him, so that he does not know the way to the city.

⸺⁶

---

16 1973-74: Season 19, Series No. 598, No. 11 in season, written by Calvin Clements, Sr.

117. "I always figger the most importantness thing fer ah feller to be, is reliableness!"

Prov. 10.5: A son who gathers in summer is prudent, but a son who sleeps in harvest brings shame.

Prov. 10.26: Like vinegar to the teeth, and smoke to the eyes, so is the sluggard to those who send him.

118. Festus is talking to two small children: "Now if ah certain fellers would happen ta keep the forge ah go'n whilst ah certain feller was shoe'n his mule, then those certain fellers might jist earn ah peppermint stick!"[17]

Prov. 11.17: A man who is kind benefits himself, but a cruel man hurts himself.

119. At the dinner table Festus is talking to a widow lady that he helped all day on her farm: "You know it's jist plain shamefulness the way I packed away them vitals the way I did!"[18]

Prov. 1.31: Therefore they shall eat the fruit of their way and be sated with their own devices.

---

[17] 1968-69: Season 14, Series No. 477, No. 14 in season, written by Wm Blinn.
[18] 1968-69: Season 14, Series No. 471, No. 8 in season, written by Calvin Clements, Sr.

Is. 61.7: Instead of your shame you shall have a double portion, instead of dishonor you shall rejoice in your lot; therefore in your land you shall possess a double portion; yours shall be everlasting joy.

Is. 49.9b-10: They shall feed along the ways, on all bare heights shall be their pasture; they shall not hunger or thirst, neither scorching wind nor sun shall smite them, for He who has pity on them will lead them, and by the springs of water will guide them.

Prov. 27.7: He who is sated loathes honey, but to one who is hungry everything bitter is sweet.

―⸺

120. Festus talks to two young boys that he forgave for stealing his money pouch when he wasn't looking: "I can see why ya done it boys, but what ya done was jist plain wrong! Don't ya boys ever do anything again ta take that pride-someness look from your momma's face!"[19]

Prov. 17.9: He who forgives an offense seeks love, but he who repeats a matter alienates a friend.

―⸺

---
[19] 1968-69: Season 14, Series No. 477, No. 14 in season, written by Wm Blinn.

121. Festus just finished helping a down-and-out farm family outside of Dodge: "Well now, so-long to ya folks, now come on Ruth lets scratch yer feet and write some gravel!"

Prov. 14.21: He who despises his neighbor is a sinner, but happy is he who is kind to the poor.

Prov. 18.19: A brother helped is like a strong city, but quarreling is like the bars of a castle.

---

122. Festus is helping an old man clear some land on his farm: "That ole tree stump was an ornery cuss an we got her better'd an batter'd, but she ain't ready ta give in yet! Come on Ruth hitch on here an we'll give her another yank!"[19.1]

Prov. 14.4: Where there are no oxen, there is no grain; but abundant crops come by the strength of the ox.

Prov. 14.22: Do they not err that devise evil? Those who devise good meet loyalty and faithfulness.

[19.1] Various sayings of Festus Haggen from Season 12, 1966-67 through Season 20, 1974-75. Wikipedia list of Gunsmoke television episodes. Last modified on 21 May 2016, at 00:59.

123. "When my friend died, I guess we all know'd it was go'n ta happen, but it sure is ah bitter pill ta swaller!"

Prov. 14.12-13: There is a way that seems right to a man, but its end is the way to death. Even in laughter the heart is sad, and the end of joy is grief.

Ecc. 9.2-3: Since one fate comes to all, to the righteous and the wicked, to the good and the evil, to the clean and the unclean, to man, so is the sinner; and he who swears is as he who shuns an oath. Thus an evil in all that is done under the sun, that one fate comes to all.

124. "Festus, look you don't have a cruel bone in your body, but I'll tell you something, you have been known to be stubborn," Matt tells him.[19.2]

Deut. 29.19: One, who, when he hears the words of this sworn covenant, blesses himself in his heart, saying, 'I shall be safe, though I walk in the stubbornness of my heart';

19.2 Ibid.

125. "Now, in New Orleans this Royal Whiskey is what we call 'Café Royal'," Dr. Chapman said. "In Dodge we call it 'Haggen Charm'," said Kitty.[20]

Prov. 27.2: Let another praise you, and not your own mouth; a stranger, and not your own lips.

⸎

126. "Ole Doc, yer talking has got ah way of cut'n ta the bone, I'll say that much fer ya!"

Prov. 18.21: Death and life are in the power of the tongue, and those who love it will eat its fruits.

Prov. 25.15: With patience a ruler may be persuaded, and a soft tongue will break a bone.

Ps. 52.2: You are plotting destruction. Your tongue is like a sharp razor, you worker of treachery.

Ps. 140.3: They make their tongue sharp as a serpent's, and under their lips is the poison of vipers.

⸎

---

[20] 1971-72: Season 17, Series No. 544, No. 5 in season, written by Jack Miller.

127. "That's ah pretty sorry excuse fer ah horse, but it orta be worth at least 40 silver dollars!"[21]

Prov. 11.1: A false balance is an abomination to
the Lord, but a just weight is his delight.

Prov. 16.11: A just balance and scales are the Lord's;
all the weights in the bag are his work.

Prov. 20.23: Diverse weights are an abomination
to the Lord, and false scales are not good.

―⸺

128. "Jist so as to ya know, the safest place ta look at an elephant is from ah long distance, an that's ah o'lee fact!"[22]

Ps. 139.2: Thou knowest when I sit down and when
I rise up; thou discernest my thoughts from afar.

―⸺

129. Festus has just completed the sale of the property and possessions of a friend who died and he, the executor of the man's meager estate, is preparing to take the

---

21 1972-73: Season 18, Series No. 571, No. 8 in season, written by Paul Savage.
22 1972-73: Season 18, Series No. 578, No. 15 in season, written by Dudley Bromley.

money that remains from the estate sale to the dead man's daughter who ran off to the city to be a saloon girl. Some folks in Dodge are ridiculing Festus for making a long trip to the city to deliver such a meager sum to the dead man's heir:

> "What I did fer her was not did fer money, and I'm fix'n ta deliver these 11 silver dollars to her in Abilene! Don't ya see?"[23]

Prov. 3.9-10: Honor the Lord with your substance and with the first fruits of all your produce; then your barns will be filled with plenty, and your vats will be bursting with wine.

Prov. 13.22: A good man leaves an inheritance to his children, but the sinner's wealth is laid up for the righteous.

Prov. 15.33: The fear of the Lord is instruction in wisdom, and humility goes before honor.

Prov. 28.22: A miserly man hastens after wealth, and does not know that want will come upon him.

---

23 1972-73: Season 18, Series No. 571, No. 8 in season, written by Paul Savage.

130. "I'm go'n ta prove ta ya folks that I'm clear up ta neck high with personableness!"

Prov. 17.17: A friend loves at all times, and
a brother is born for adversity.

Prov. 19.11: Good sense makes a man slow to anger,
and it is his glory to overlook an offense.

—⁂—

131. Festus adds on to a prayer at the dinner table of a widow and her boys who are soon expecting the arrival of a man she is to marry and has never seen before: "Oh, and Lord if ya want ta make the feller ah might bit more looksomer than some feller that ain't go'n ta be named sit'n at this table, ya shore won't git no fuss'n from folks around these here parts. Amen."[23.1]

Prov. 22.4: The reward for humility and fear
of the Lord is riches and honor and life.

Prov. 31.10, 23: A good wife who can find? She is far more precious than jewels. Her husband is known in the gates, when he sits among the elders of the land.

—⁂—

[23.1] Various sayings of Festus Haggen from Season 12, 1966-67 through Season 20, 1974-75. Wikipedia list of Gunsmoke television episodes. Last modified on 21 May 2016, at 00:59.

132. "Watch what yer do'n ya knucklehead!"

Prov. 15.3: The eyes of the Lord are in every place, keeping watch on the evil and the good.

―✺―

133. Festus tells the posse: "Now if them scoundrels double back on us, ya jist squeeze off ah couple of shots an we'll come ah run'n!"[23.2]

Prov. 11.3: The integrity of the upright guides them, but the crookedness of the treacherous destroys them.

2Thes. 2.3: Let no one deceive you in any way; for that day will not come, unless the rebellion comes first, and the man of lawlessness is revealed, the son of perdition.

―✺―

134. "When it comes ta help'n folks, somehow, someday, an maybe er the most left-handed words in ole Websterber's dicterinary!"

Prov. 6.9-11: How long will you lie there, O sluggard? When will you arise from your sleep? A little sleep, a little slumber,

---

[23.2] 1973-74: Season 19, Series No. 590, No. 3 in season, written by Ron Bishop.

a little folding of the hands to rest, and poverty will come upon you like a vagabond, and want like an armed man.

Prov. 26.15-16: A sluggard buries his hand in the dish; it wears him out to bring it back to his mouth. The sluggard is wiser in his own eyes than seven men who can answer discreetly.

―⸺

135. "I don't believe I can help ya Percy Crump. It seems that if somebody orta'd ta dug two graves up there at the cementerary there's got ta be ah body around here someplace don't ya think?"[23.3]

Ps. 49.14: Like sheep they are appointed for Sheol; Death shall be their shepherd; straight to the grave they descend, and their form shall waste away; Sheol shall be their home.

―⸺

136. "Mathew, ya know those two graves dug up there on Boot Hill? Well I rode ole Ruth up there ta take ah gander round, an one of them graves ain't empty no more!"

23.3 Various sayings of Festus Haggen from Season 12: 1966-67 through Season 20, 1974-75. Wikipedia list of Gunsmoke television episodes. Last modified on 21 May 2016, at 00:59.

1Cor. 15.55: "O death, where is thy victory?
O death, where is thy sting?"

⸙

137. "It's hard ta say what those kill'n side washers will do!"

Ex. 20.1,13: "Thou shall not murder."

⸙

138. "Me an ole Ruth has been have'n ah look-see out east of town and it's quieter'n ah ghost on ah dark night. Now I'm go'n on down yonder ta the depot and take ah quick look-see!"[23.4]

Ecc. 4.6: Better is a handful of quietness than two hands full of toil and a striving after the wind.

Job 10.21-22: "Before I go whence I shall not return, to the land of gloom and deep darkness, the land of gloom and chaos, where light is as darkness."

Job 24.16-17: "In the dark they dig through houses; by day they shut themselves up; they do not know the

---

23.4 Ibid.

light. For deep darkness is morning to all of them; for they are friends with the terrors of deep darkness."

—⁂—

139. "I thought you went hunting," Doc says to Festus. "I did," Festus tells him, and Doc replies, "Well why did you come back?" "I got done hunt'n ya ole scallywag!"(Festus).[23.5]

> Ps. 116.7: Return, O my soul, to your rest; for the Lord has dealt bountifully with you.

—⁂—

140. Festus sees two children he hasn't seen in quite a spell: "Well howdy young'ns, look at ya. Every time I see'd ya both, I swear ya've grow'd more than knee high to ah grassityhopper. And look at ya little girl, now ain't ya the prettiestsome thing I've ever saw. And you little feller, ya ain't noth'n but freckles, worts, and feet!"[24]

> Matt. 19.13-14: Then children were brought to him that he might lay his hands on them and pray. The disciples rebuked the people; But Jesus said, "Let the children come to me, and do not hinder them; for to such belongs the kingdom of heaven."

23.5 Ibid.
24 1968-69: Season 14, Series No. 477, No. 14 in season, written by Wm. Blinn.

Prov. 22.6: Train up a child in the way he should go,
and when he is old he will not depart from it.

―∽―

141. "A feller has ta git out'a town now an then jist ta git away from all the hub-bub!"

Ps. 23.2-3: He makes me lie down in green pastures.
He leads me beside still waters; he restores my soul.

Job 3.17: "There the wicked cease from
troubling, and there the weary are at rest."

Job 11.18: "And you will have confidence, because there is
hope; you will be protected and take your rest in safety."

―∽―

142. "Have ya ever saw the likes of this weather? Why it's hotter'n ah depot stove!"

Ps. 107.4: Some wandered in desert wastes,
finding no way to a city to dwell in; hungry and
thirsty, their soul fainted within them.

―∽―

143. "I'll tell ya Mathew, it's enough ta make ah preacher curse ah blue streak, and it puts me into ah foam'n fit. He don't think of noth'n and nobody cept'n his ownself. Someth'ns got ta be did and I mean did now, and that's ah fact!"[24.1]

Prov. 25.28: A man without self-control is like a city broken into and left without walls.

Prov. 27.12: A prudent man sees danger and hides himself; but the simple go on, and suffer for it.

Phil. 2.3-4: Do nothing from selfishness or conceit, but in humility count others better than yourselves. Let each of you look not only to his own interests, but also to the interests of others.

---

144. "Now that don't sound like ah horse race between two ranch ponies ta me, someth'ns mighty fishy go'n on!"[25]

Ecc. 9.11-12: Again, I saw that under the sun the race is not to the swift, nor the battle to the strong, nor bread to the wise, nor riches to the intelligent, nor

---

24.1 Various sayings of Festus Haggen from Season 12, 1966-67 through Season 20, 1974-75. Wikipedia list of Gunsmoke television episodes. Last modified on 21 May 2016, at 00:59.
25 1972-73: Season 18, Series No. 577, No. 14 in season, written by Jack Freeman.

favor to the men of skill; but time and chance happen to them all. For man does not know his time. Like fish that are taken in an evil net, and like birds that are caught in a snare, so the sons of men are snared at an evil time, when it suddenly falls upon them.

---

145. "I bet ya that ole Ruth can beat yer fancy horse in ah race between yer place and town!"[26]

> 1Cor. 9.24: Do you not know that in a race all the runners compete, but only one receives the prize? So run that you may obtain it.

---

146. "Catfish got'a be cleaned quick, otherwise they'll sour on ya. Everybody knows that Doc!"

> Is. 19.5, 8: And the waters of the Nile will be dried up, and the river will be parched and dry; The fishermen will mourn and lament, all who cast hook in the Nile; and they will languish who spread nets upon the water.

---

26 Ibid.

Prov. 18.14: A man's spirit will endure sickness,
but a broken spirit who can bear?

---

147. "Matt! There is no such thing as ONLY a picnic when there's a women involved," Doc says.

Prov. 31.29: "Many women have done
excellently, but you surpass them all."

---

148. "It'll take ah heap more than the likes of ya scallywags ta take over this town!"

Prov. 24.10-11: If you faint in the day of adversity, your strength is small. Rescue those who are being taken away to death; hold back those who are stumbling to the slaughter.

---

149. "All right folks, ya heard what Mathew said, now git off'n the street an move along back home, before some of ya gits hurt or killt in this here fracas!"[26.1]

[26.1] Various sayings of Festus Haggen from Season 12, 1966-67 through Season 20, 1974-75. Wikipedia list of Gunsmoke television episodes. Last modified on 21 May 2016, at 00:59.

Ps. 27.5: For he will hide me in his shelter in the
day of trouble, he will conceal me under the cover
of his tent, he will set me high upon a rock.

―⁂―

150. "Sam, draw me another beer would ya, Doc'll settle-up with ya later!"

Prov. 19.4: Wealth brings many new friends,
but a poor man is deserted by his friend.

―⁂―

151. "What time is it Doc?" Why don't you get yourself a watch," says Doc. "Ah fiddle I'd feel silly carry'n one of them things around. Watches was invented fer doctors an lawyers an such as that, not fer us Haggens!"[26.2]

Ecc. 3.1: For everything there is a season, and
a time for every matter under heaven.

Ecc. 8.6: For every matter has its time and way,
although man's trouble lies heavy upon him.

Ezek. 3.27: "But when I speak with you, I will open your
mouth, and you shall say to them, 'Thus says the Lord

26.2 Ibid.

God'; he that will hear, let him hear; and he that will refuse to hear, let him refuse; for they are a rebellious house.

---

152. "Yer ah spout'n off pretty big fer such ah litter feller!"[27]

Prov. 27.1-2: Do not boast about tomorrow, for you do not know what a day may bring forth. Let another praise you, and not your own mouth; a stranger, and not your own lips.

---

153. "Ya don't think he'll haul off an do someth'n silly do ya Mathew? Of course he's got his ole ears splayed back and his eye-balls pooched out and roll'n around like he's squared-off at ya like ya was some blood enemy, when ya been friends fer the biggerest part of yer life. Maybe we orta jist collect him and slap him in the cooler'n box fer ah spell till he simmers down!"[27.1]

Prov. 24.25: But those who rebuke the wicked will have delight, and a good blessing will be upon them.

---

27 1972-73: Season 18, Series No. 578, No. 15 in season, written by Dudley Bromley.
27.1 Various sayings of Festus Haggen from Season 12, 1966-67 through Season 20, 1974-75. Wikipedia list of Gunsmoke television episodes. Last modified on 21 May 2016, at 00:59.

Ps. 5.10: Make them bear their guilt, O God; let them fall by their own counsels; because of their many transgressions cast them out, for they have rebelled against thee.

---

154. A couple of outlaws denied to Doc that they had anything to do with shooting a fellow and Festus says: "Well Doc, course what would they say? Ya don't expect em ta fess up and put their necks in the ringer do ya? I sure don't like the looks a'things a'tall!"[27.2]

Prov. 30.8: Remove far from me falsehood and lying; give me neither poverty nor riches; feed me with the food that is needful for me,

Ps. 62.4: They only plan to thrust him down from his eminence. They take pleasure in falsehood. They bless with their mouths, but inwardly they curse.

---

155. "Well he could jist dust his self off an take care of business till this chivalree is over an then jist dust out'a town!"

[27.2] Ibid.

Prov. 14.16: A wise man is cautious and turns away from evil, but a fool throws off restraint and is careless.

Prov. 30.8: Remove far from me falsehood and lying; give me neither poverty nor riches; feed me with the food that is needful for me,

---

156. "Of all the clabborated dribble come'n out'a yer tater-trap. It darned near come ta the top ah my boots. Come on silver tongue it's time ta go!"[28]

Is. 5.18: Woe to those who draw iniquity with cords of falsehood, who draw sin as with cart ropes,

Ezek. 13.6: "They have spoken falsehood and divined a lie; they say, 'Says the Lord,' when the Lord has not sent them, and yet they expect Him to fulfill their word."

---

157. "Yer about as sincere as ah undertaker at ah five dollar funeral!"

---

28 1966-67: Season 12, Series No. 414, No. 5 in season, written by James Landis.

158. "I git ah little bone here on the back ah my neck, jist starts hurt'n like thunder when they's trouble brew'n. It's jaw'n on me pretty good right now!"[28.1]

> Job 15.35: "They conceive mischief and bring forth evil and their heart prepares deceit."

> Jer. 9.5: "Everyone deceives his neighbor, and no one speaks the truth; they have taught their tongue to speak lies; they commit iniquity and are too weary to repent."

> Eph. 5.6: Let no one deceive you with empty words, for it is because of these things that the wrath of God comes upon the sons of disobedience.

159. "Yer sleep'n yer dang life away. Git up off'n yer backside an find yerself ah pay'n job!"

> Prov. 6.9-11: How long will you lie there, O sluggard? When will you arise from your sleep? A little sleep, a little slumber, a little folding of the hands to rest, and poverty will come upon you like a vagabond, and want like an armed man.

28.1 1967-68: Season 13, Series No. 457, No. 19 in season, written by Hal Sitowitz.

Prov. 24.33: A little sleep, a little slumber, a little folding of the hands to rest, and poverty will come upon you like a robber, and want like an armed man.

―♾―

160. "Don't stay up there ah flatter'n yer gums, come on down here an lets git ah go'n!"

Prov. 4.24: Put away from you crooked speech, and put devious talk far from you.

Job 11.2-3: "Should a multitude of words go unanswered; and a man full of talk be vindicated? Should your babble silence men, and when you mock, shall no one shame you?"

―♾―

161. "Ya look ah mighty new looksome person in our town Miss, I'll tell ya that. I'll tell ya Doc that lady is ah mess of proper classomeness. If'n I was sixteen years younger, I'd be look'n in on her!"[28.2]

Prov. 6.25: Do not desire her beauty in your heart, and do not let her capture you with her eyelashes; for a harlot may be hired for a loaf of bread, but an adulteress stalks a man's very life.

28.2 Various sayings of Festus Haggen from Season 12: 1966-67 through Season 20, 1974-75. Wikipedia list of Gunsmoke television episodes. Last modified on 21 May 2016, at 00:59.

Prov. 31.17-18: She girds her loins with strength and makes
her arms strong. She perceives that her merchandise
is profitable. Her lamp does not go out at night.

—⁂—

162. "When ya go'n ta git it through yer thick head, ya jist can't go up an steal someth'n! The onlyest thing ya got'a do is ask ta borry it!"

Prov. 6.30: Do not men despise a thief if he steals
to satisfy his appetite when he is hungry?

Prov. 22.22: Do not rob the poor, because he is poor,
or crush the afflicted at the gate, for the Lord will plead
their cause and despoil of life those who despoil them.

Ex. 20.15: "Thou shall not steal."

—⁂—

163. "The law says ya don't orta be hang'n ah feller fer try'n ta do right!"

Ps. 119.153: Look on my affliction and deliver
me, for I do not forget thy law.

Ex. 20.16: "You shall not bear false witness against your neighbor.

Prov. 14.5: A faithful witness does not lie, but a false witness breathes out lies.

⚬

164. "Hi there Newly!" "How ya doing Festus," Newly asks. "Well this place is lonesome'ner than ah graveyard at midnight." Newly asks, "How about some coffee?" "No, the onlyest thing I want ta do is ta git some sleep, unless ya want me ta stay here an jawbone with ya fer awhile."[28.2]

Prov. 3.24: If you sit down, you will not be afraid; when you lie down, your sleep will be sweet.

⚬

165. "Mathew, I've done enough this morn'n ta sprain an owl's head!"

Prov. 14.6: A scoffer seeks wisdom in vain, but knowledge is easy for a man of understanding.

28.2 1972-73: Season 18, Series No. 578, No. 15 in season, written by Dudley Bromley.

Ecc. 12.12: My son, beware of anything beyond these. Of making many books there is no end, and much study is a weariness of the flesh.

Ps. 19.1-2: The heavens are telling the glory of God; and the firmament proclaims his handiwork. Day to day pours forth speech, and night to night declares knowledge.

---

166. "Young'n, it wouldn't hurt ya none ta not be so short mouthed with yer elders, besides what in tarnation are ya do'n way out here in the middle of no place. This ain't no country for ah girl ta be all by her ownself!"[29]

Prov. 10.19: When words are many, transgression is not lacking, but he who restrains his lips is prudent.

---

167. "Doc, I know ah heap more of that whole bad outfit than anybody needs ta know!"

Prov. 15.2: The tongue of the wise dispenses knowledge, but the mouths of fools pour out folly.

---

[29] 1974-75: Season 20, Series No. 629, No. 18 in season, written by Herman Groves.

Prov. 14.6: A scoffer seeks wisdom in vain, but knowledge is easy for a man of understanding.

---

168. "I'm look'n fer ah feller, an he's a quick tempered skag an ah vicious-some killer!"

Prov. 14.17-19: A man of quick temper acts foolishly, but a man of discretion is patient. The simple acquire folly, but the prudent are crowned with knowledge. The evil bow down before the good, and the wicked at the gates of the righteous.

---

169. "When that fight broke out last night in the Long Branch I thought ya'd fold like a bad hand, but ya hang'd in there tighter'n a tick!"

Prov. 24.17-18: Do not rejoice when your enemy falls, and let not your heart be glad when he stumbles; lest the Lord see it, and be displeased, and turn away his anger from him.

Mic. 7.8: Rejoice not over me, O my enemy; when I fall, I shall rise; when I sit in darkness, the Lord will be a light to me.

2Sam. 22.40-41: For thou didst gird me with strength for the battle; thou didst make my assailants sink under me. Thou didst make my enemies turn their backs to me, those who hated me, and I destroyed them.

---

170. "Call'n it ah night are ya," Festus asks a friend. "Ya! If I don't get home before 11 o'clock the wife starts worry'n."[29.1]

Ecc. 8.6: For every matter has its time and way, although man's trouble lies heavy upon him.

---

171. Matt tells Festus, "Festus, I want you to round up some men we can trust like Lathrop, Halligan, Burk, and Potter!" Festus replies, "Mathew, ole Halligan he's got the argu someth'n fierce. He can't hardly even git out of bed, and ya know that Mr. Potter gots that there bad sick girl that can't be left by her ownself, but I'll git everybody I can muster!"[30]

Prov. 25.19: Trust in faithless men in time of trouble is like a bad tooth or a foot that slips.

29.1 1974-75: Season 20, Series No. 619, No. 8 in season, written by Jim Byrnes.
30 Ibid.

172. "Festus, get that body over to Percy Crumps' place," Matt says. "Rightly promptly Mathew. Burk, Lathrop, ya other fellers come on over here an git ah hold of him now! All right come on now git ah move on, we ain't got all night, don't ya see?"

Ecc. 8.10: Then I saw the wicked buried; they used to go in and out of the holy place, and were praised in the city where they had done such things. This also is vanity.

Jer. 21.8: "And to this people you shall say: 'Thus says the Lord: Behold, I set before you the way of life and the way of death.'"

Rev. 20.12: And I saw the dead, great and small, standing before the throne, and books were opened. Also another book was opened, which is the book of life. And the dead were judged by what was written in the books, by what they had done.

༺

173. "How's Doc Adams," Judge Kendall asks Festus. "Pfftt, that ole scudder? Same as always, stubborn'er my mule! Here judge, I'll take yer things on over to the Dodge House fer ya!"[31]

---

31 1974-75: Season 20, Series No. 621, No. 10 in season, written by Wm. Keys.

Ps. 81.12: So I gave them over to their stubborn hearts, to follow their own counsels.

―⸺

174. "There they are! That's their horses! What do ya want us ta do Mathew?" "Festus, you head around back of the farmhouse and Newly and I will call em out when we're ready!"[31.1]

Ps. 83.14-15: As fire consumes the forest, as the flame sets the mountains ablaze, so do thou pursue them with thy tempest and terrify them with thy hurricane.

Lam. 3.66: "Thou wilt pursue them in anger and destroy them from under thy heavens, O Lord."

Jer. 29.18: "I will pursue them with sword, famine, and pestilence, and will make them a horror to all the kingdoms of the earth, to be a curse, a terror, a hissing, and a reproach among all the nations where I have driven them.

―⸺

31.1 Ibid.

175. "Don't try it young'n! Ya ain't no more an ah step an ah half from ah hole in the ground right now!"[31.2]

> Jas. 1.3: "Let no one say when he is tempted, 'I am tempted by God', for God cannot be tempted with evil and he himself temps no one."

---

176. A prisoner asks, "Who might this be in the fine cloth?" Festus says, "That's the man that's fix'n ta hang ya!"[32]

> Ezek. 36.19: I scattered them among the nations, and they were dispersed through the countries; in accordance with their conduct and their deeds I judged them.

> Is. 66.16: For by fire will the Lord execute judgment, and by his sword, upon all flesh; and those slain by the Lord shall be many.

> Deut. 1.16: And I charged your judges at that time, "Hear the cases between your brethren, and judge righteously between a man and his brother or the alien that is with him.

31.2 Ibid.
32 Ibid.

177. "I've had ta done ah lot of things in my life, but release'n that trash from jail goes agin my grain!"[33]

Ecc. 1.15: What is crooked cannot be made straight,
and what is lacking cannot be numbered.

Prov. 17.9: He who forgives an offense seeks love,
but he who repeats a matter alienates a friend.

Ezek. 7.22-23: "I will turn my face from them, that they may profane my precious place; robbers shall enter and profane it, and make desolation. Because the land is full of bloody crimes and the city is full of violence."

178. "I slept with one eye open all night after I saw yer rattlesnake friend, and this here breakfast lizard meat is darn awful stringy!"[34]

Prov. 30.28: The lizard you can take in your
hands, yet it is in kings' palaces.

---

33 1966-67: Season 12, Series No. 414, No. 5 in season, written by James Landis.
34 1974-75: Season 20, Series No. 622, No. 11 in season, written by Jim Byrnes.

179. "Are ya go'n ta stand there squaller'n til yer ole tongue gits so swolled up it chokes yer wind off, er ya come'n with me?"[35]

Ps. 5.8: Lead me, O Lord, in thy righteousness because of my enemies; make thy way straight before me.

Ps. 34.12: What man is there who desires life, and covets many days, that he may enjoy good?

180. "Ya got about as much chance as ah rat between ah dog's teeth!"[36]

Jer. 22.30: Thus says the Lord: "Write this man down as childless, a man who shall not succeed in his days: for none of his offspring shall succeed in sitting on the throne of David, and ruling again in Judah."

Joel 2.32: And it shall come to pass that all who call upon the name of the Lord shall be delivered; for in Mount Zion and in Jerusalem there shall be those who escape, as the Lord has said, and among the survivors shall be those whom the Lord calls.

---

35 1974-75: Season 20, Series No. 623, No. 12 in season, written by Jim Byrnes.
36 Ibid.

Prov. 27.12: Sensible people will see trouble coming and avoid it, but an unthinking person will walk right into it and regret it later.

―❦―

181. "Yer colder'n a witch's kiss aren't ya!"[37]

Prov. 17.20: A man of crooked mind does not prosper, and one with a perverse tongue falls into calamity.

―❦―

182. "Yer cheat'n partner friend is dead! He died in 1859! This is 1873 and ya been out yonder in this here desert all these years ah hate'n ah dead person!"[38]

―❦―

183. "Is that what ya call bad luck, cheat'n people an get'n caught at it?"[38.1]

Prov. 19.7: All a poor man's brothers hate him; how much more do his friends go far from him! He pursues them with words, but does not have them.

---

37 Ibid.
38 Ibid.
38.1 1968-69: Season 14, Series No. 481, No. 18 in season, written by Calvin Clements, Sr.

Ps. 25.19: Consider how many are my foes, and
with what violent hatred they hate me.

Ps. 26.5: I hate the company of evildoers,
and I will not sit with the wicked.

Ps. 119.113: I hate double-minded men, but I love thy law.

Is. 63.17: O Lord, why dost thou make us err from thy ways
and harden our heart, so that we fear thee not? Return
for the sake of thy servants, the tribes of thy heritage.

Prov. 29.25: The fear of man lays a snare,
but he who trusts in the Lord is safe.

―⚬―

184. "Well now it's hard ta figger Mathew. From here on these foot tracks is scattered worse an ah herd of spooked cattle. They sure won't be git'n too far on foot. We'd orta catch em before days out Matthew!"

Prov. 21.16: A man who wanders from the way of
understanding will rest in the assembly of the dead.

―⚬―

185. "That's our money yer take'n," Says one of the bank robbers. Festus says, "Yer money? Seems ta me it's Wells Fargo money!"[39]

Prov. 29.24: A partner of a thief hates his own life;
he hears the curse, but discloses nothing.

Ps. 50.19: You give your mouth free reign for
evil, and your tongue frames deceit.

---

186. "His horse come ah wonder'n in here ta camp ah couple hours ago. Wonder'd whose it was," says a Hide Skinner. "But ya jist didn't wonder enough ta go ah look'n fer whose it was did ya," says Festus.[40]

Ps. 18.41: They cried for help, but there was none to save,
they cried to the Lord, but he did not answer them.

Ps. 68.21: But God will shatter the heads of his enemies,
the hairy crown of him who walks in his guilty ways.

---

[39] 1969-70: Season 15, Series No. 509, No. 20 in season, written by Jim Byrnes.
[40] 1974-75: Season 20, Series No. 626, No. 15 in season, written by Paul Savage.

187. "It ain't gonna hurt none if I take ah look-see around now is it," Festus asks. "No ya can't! Don't want ya poke'n around my camp," says the Hide Skinner!" "This here badge says I am, and I'm go'n ta do jist that! Mister ya ain't put upon a'tall yet! Not by me, now step back before ya git me riled up!"[41]

Tit. 3.1: Remind them to be submissive to rulers and authorities, to be obedient, to be ready for any honest work,

⸺

188. "I'll tell ya young'n, if ya keep stuff'n them vitals away like that, yer go'n ta git so blamed fat ya can't stand up on yer feet by yer ownself. Don't ya see?"[41.1]

Prov. 23.1: When you sit down to eat with a ruler, observe carefully what is before you; and put a knife to your throat if you are a man given to appetite.

Prov. 23.6-8: Do not eat the bread of a man who is stingy; do not desire his delicacies, for he is like one who is inwardly reckoning. "Eat and drink!" he says to you; but his heart is not with you. You will vomit up the morsels which you have eaten, and waste your pleasant words.

⸺

---
41 Ibid.
41.1 Various sayings of Festus Haggen from Season 12: 1966-67 through Season 20, 1974-75. Wikipedia list of Gunsmoke television episodes. Last modified on 21 May 2016, at 00:59.

189. "Best thing they is ta thank ah friend is ta jist divy up with him. Don't ya see?"

Prov. 16.11: A just balance and scales are the Lord's; all the weights in the bag are his work.

Prov.20.23: Diverse weights are an abomination to the Lord, and false scales are not good.

―⸮―

190. Doc says to Matt, "Every once in awhile Festus does something that turns out all right Matt. Now if you tell him I said that, I'll deny it!" "I won't say a word," says Matt.[41.2]

Jas.4.17: Whoever knows what is right to do and fails to do it, for him it is sin.

1Jn. 2.29: If you know that he is righteous, you may be sure that everyone who does right is born of him.

―⸮―

41.2 Ibid.

191. "Newly, if ya hadn't really went ta work an tied the can ta the bulls tail, I haven't never saw it did. Ya did as fast as wall's clock on him right sure!"

Prov. 22.29: Do you see a man skillful in his work? He will stand before kings; he will not stand before obscure men.

Prov. 13.16: In everything a prudent man acts with knowledge, but a fool flaunts his folly.

Prov. 27.2: Let another praise you, and not your own mouth; a stranger, and not your own lips.

⸻

192. "HOLD IT! Move one inch an yer dead!"

Deut. 30.15: "See, I have set before you this day life and good, death and evil."

⸻

193. "Ya know that other preacher back there in Nestatoga? He could spout off the Bible like it was ah new well," says Festus to a Preacher. "Festus, I learned a long time ago that spending the time to memorize the

Bible would be better spent trying to do what it recommended," says the Preacher.[42]

Job. 11.2-3: "Should a multitude of words go unanswered, and a man full of talk be vindicated? Should your babble silence men, and when you mock, shall no one shame you?"

Job 15.2-3: "Should a wise man answer with windy knowledge, and fill him self with the east wind? Should he argue in unprofitable talk, or in words with which he can do no good?"

―⁓―

194. "What er ya sit'n up in the middle of the night read'n there Reverend," Festus asks. "I'm reading about a man named Ahab who was trying to catch a whale." "Ya mean one oh them great big ole fish that lives in the ocean?" "Yes, a white one." "White? I'll be Bill! Do tell! Well did he catch it? Did that feller Ahab catch that white whale that he was ah fish'n fer?" "Yes he did, but of course it killed him." "Appears ta me if ah preacher wants ta read about whales he orta be satisfied with read'n about ole Jonah an his tribe in the Bible! Leastwise that there'n had ah happy end'n!"[43]

---

[42] 1974-75: Season 20, Series No. 632, No. 21 in season, written by Wm. Putman.
[43] Ibid.

Jonah 2.10: And the Lord spoke to the fish, and
it vomited out Jonah upon the dry land.

—⸙—

195. "If that don't make ya dip yer snuff. Ten O them dollars was my gold piece I loaned him that he went an lost in that blamed poker game! He orta soak his head in Squaw Creek an cool off!"[44]

Pro. 14.17-19: A man of quick temper acts foolishly, but a man of discretion is patient. The simple acquire folly, but the prudent are crowned with knowledge. The evil bow down before the good, the wicked bow at the gates of the righteous.

—⸙—

196. "Now if that don't tie the pup!"

Prov. 11.13: He who goes about as a talebearer reveals secrets, but he who is trustworthy in spirit keeps a thing hidden.

—⸙—

197. "I could track ah man's hoof tracks through a buffalo stampede, an that's an o'lee fact!"

---

[44] 1966-67: Season 12, Series No. 416, No. 7 in season, written by Robert Lewin.

Job 19.22: "Why do you, like God, pursue me? Why are you not satisfied with my flesh?"

Lam. 3.66: "Thou wilt pursue them in anger and destroy them from under thy heavens, O Lord."

―⸺

198. "You were right Mathew, that little scamp is up to someth'n. Jist ah minute er two ago he bought his self ah ticket clean ta Calyforny!" "Keep an eye on things here will you," Matt asks Festus." "I'll do it Mathew, don't ya worry about noth'n!"[44.1]

Ps. 124.7: We have escaped as a bird from the snare of the fowlers; the snare is broken, and we have escaped!

―⸺

199. "THERE! RIGHT THERE! Mathew, how much is them boots here in the catalog?" "Well Festus, they are $5 a pair." "Five dollars? They orta be arrested ask'n ah price like that! Don't ya see Doc?" Then Doc asks Festus, "You paying for the beers for once are you Festus?" Festus says to Doc, "Well it's yer turn ta buy ain't it Doc?" "NO," says Doc. "Well you stingy ole skin flint! I

44.1 1973-74: Season 19, Series No. 609, No. 22 in season, written by Jim Byrnes.

recollect fair is fair. Mathew bought the first round, Miss Kitty bought the second one and now it's yer turn!"[44.2]

Ps. 112.5: It is well with the man who deals generously and lends, who conducts his affairs with justice.

Ps. 112.9: He has distributed freely, he has given to the poor; his righteousness endures forever; his horn is exalted in honor.

---

200. "Mathew, here's that teletygram from Spearville. That's one man's tater trap ah jammer'n there in the jail say'n he's not guilty! What's it say?" "Well he's right, it says he's not guilty, claims self defense," Matt tells Festus. "WHAT? Ya mean ta tell me now ya got'a go out there an meet that Tramlin gang on account of that no-good feller there in jail?"[44.3]

Ps. 68.21: But God will shatter the heads of his enemies, the hairy crown of him who walks in his guilty ways.

Is. 50.9: Behold, the Lord God helps me; who will declare me guilty? Behold, all them will wear out like a garment; the moth will eat them up.

[44.2] 1968-69: Season 14, Series No. 469, No. 6 in season, written by Ron Bishop.
[44.3] Ibid.

201. "Festus, you mind riding out to the Bishop place and tell him his prize bull has arrived in Dodge," asks Burk from the freight office. "Burk, I'd like ta hep ya out, but with Mathew outa town I got my deputy'n duties ta be took care of."[45]

Prov. 4.23: Keep your heart with all vigilance;
for from it flow the springs of life.

Ecc. 11.4: He who observes the wind will not sow;
and he who regards the clouds will not reap.

Is. 1.19: If you are willing and obedient,
you shall eat the good of the land.

202. "Ya jist wait ah minute! Yer git'n the blamed wagon before the mule on this reward thing, ya knucklehead! We'll wait an see what Mathew says on it when he gits back from Hays!"[46]

Prov. 19.6: Many seek the favor of a generous man,
and every one is a friend to a man who gives gifts.

---

45 1969-70: Season 15, Series No. 497, No. 8 in season, written by Calvin Clements Sr.
46 1968-69: Season 14, Series No. 467, No. 4 in season, written by Calvin Clements Sr..

Is. 40.10: Behold, the Lord God comes with might, and his arm rules for him; behold, his reward is with him, and his recompense before him.

―⸺

203. "Good morn'n Merry Florene! How's the teacher'n come'n at yer school house?" Merry says, "Jist fine Mr. Festus!" Festus replies, "You'd be jist plumed surprised ta here how many good folks is say'n about yer teacher'n. Why I hear'd folks say they ain't no sense in send'n fer ah new teacher, cause Merry Florene is ah do'n so good!" Merry asks Festus, "Is that the truth Mr. Festus?" "Course it is. Wouldn't surprise me none if you's ta be git'n asked ta be the regular school marm fer Dodge!"[47]

Prov. 22.6: Train up a child in the way he should go, and when he is old he will not depart from it.

Prov. 9.9: Give instruction to a wise man, and he will be still wiser; teach a righteous man and he will increase in learning.

Prov. 1.8: Hear, my son, your father's instructions, and reject not your mother's teaching; for they are a fair garland for your head, and pendants for your neck.

---

47 1969-70: Season 15, Series No. 497, No. 8 in season, written by Calvin Clements Sr.

Lk. 6.40: A disciple is not above his teacher, but everyone when he is fully taught will be like his teacher.

---

204. "Yer jist ah mule in ah horse harness an yer not fool'n nobody!"[48]

Prov. 13.16: In everything a prudent man acts with knowledge, but a fool flaunts his folly.

Prov. 14.7: Leave the presence of a fool, for there you do not meet words of knowledge.

Prov. 24.7: Wisdom is too high for a fool; in the gate he does not open his mouth.
Prov. 26.1: Like snow in summer or rain in harvest, so honor is not fitting for a fool.

---

205. "Mathew, yer not gonna believe this, but they's ah buffalo out yonder in Dodge's Main Street an that ain't all neither, they's three fellers hog-tied on top of ah wagon he's roped up to!"

---

48 Ibid.

2Thes. 2.7: For the mystery of lawlessness is
already at work, only he who now restrains it
will do so until he is out of the way.

Job 21.34: "How then will you comfort me with empty nothings? There is nothing left of your answers but falsehood."

206. "I can see yer jaws ah flap'n, but I can't hear noth'n outa my ears!"

Prov. 4.24: Put away from you crooked speech,
and put devious talk far from you.

Prov. 20.19: He who goes about gossiping reveals secrets; therefore do not associate with one who speaks foolishly.

CHAPTER 2

Festus' Conversations & Encounters With Supporting Proverbs & Bible Passages[49]

---

1. Falsely Accused[50]: A farmer (Ben) was caught up in a falsified horse rustling charge, prison break, and alleged murder of a prison guard. Ben was caught and convicted with false witness testimony by Garth Brakus (a wealthy land grabbing rancher) and sentenced to life in prison. His wife (Elizabeth) came to Dodge City and helped Ben break from jail before he could be transported back to prison in Hays, Kansas. They hightailed it out of Dodge in their horse and buggy and stayed off the main roads by sticking to the prairie and rolling hills and swales. Matt and Festus know Ben is innocent, but cannot prove it. They ride out after him: **"Them tracks er as plain as the sun on ah summer sky Mathew!"** "Yeah, I can see that," says Matt. **You take that way down the dry wash and I'll take the other way and maybe we'll come across them!" "OK Mathew, see ya directly!"**

---

[49] Various conversations by Festus Haggen from Season 12: 1966-67 through Season 20, 1974-75. List of Gunsmoke television episodes in color: Wikipedia.com last modified on 21 May 2016, at 00:59.
[50] 1971-72: Season 17, Series No. 555, No. 16 in season, written by Richard Fielder.

Ex. 20.16: "You shall not bear false witness against your neighbor."

Prov. 14.5: A faithful witness does not lie, but a false witness breathes out lies.

Prov. 30.8: Remove far from me falsehood and lying; give me neither poverty nor riches; feed me with the food that is needful for me.

―❦―

Festus came upon Ben & Elizabeth holed up behind some thick brush in a dry gulch: **"Hold er right there Ben, don't be ah try'n anything silly! Now put that gun down slow an drop er right there an step away over there by yer wife!" "Festus, I told ya that I'm innocent and I'm not going with you and spend the rest of my life in prison. I'm not leaving dear Elizabeth amongst those ranch grab'n murderers to die on this dusty prairie!" Festus tells him, "I know what yer ah think'n, but put that gun down before somebody gits killed! Jist put it away from point'n at me! Don't ya see?"**

After some pleading by Festus, Ben put his gun down. Festus is talking softly as he turns his back and walks away off into the dry gulch to fetch his mule Ruth. He mounts up and rides slowly off in the opposite direction, talking to himself. Ben & Elizabeth are stunned that Festus leave them to go on their way. **"I'll tell ya, I'm fix'n ta go up ta that there prison my ownself an talk ta all them fellas I can about that there killed guard one of these days. Whenever Mathew gives me ah day er two off. Suppose'n I won't be git'n that day off any time too soon."**

Job. 4.7-8: "Think now, who that was innocent ever perished? Or where were the upright cut off? As I have seen, those who plow inequity and sow trouble reap the same."

Job 17.8-9: "Upright men are appalled at this, and the innocent stirs himself up against the godless. Yet the righteous holds to his way, and he that has clean hands grows stronger and stronger."

―♾―

Festus meets up with Matt farther on down the edge of the dry wash and they look up, and there on a ridge they sight Ben and Elizabeth in their buggy moving up over the ridge in the far distant west heading out of Kansas: **"Whoa Ruth! Howdy Mathew!" "What happened Festus?" "Well funny thing Mathew, I never could find that feller Ben that stolt all them there horses!"** "Yeah, I kind of figured that maybe we wouldn't with that head start they had on us," says Matt. **"Oh yeah, they did have a whopp'n big head start on us all right. I jist don't believe we could ever ah catched up with em! Do you Mathew?"** "Festus, I think you're right! Let's head back to town!" **"Yeah, let's make** tracks fer Dodge fer ah cold beer! I'm buy'n," Festus says with a big grin on his face.

Prov. 3.27: Do not hold good from those to whom it is due, when it is in your power to do it.

Prov. 19.9: A false witness will not go unpunished, and he who utters lies will perish.

In the Long Branch saloon back in Dodge: **"Miss Kitty, I found this letter slipped under the back door. It is addressed to you,"** says Sam the bartender. "Well, let's see what it is all about. Well what do you know, looks like Dodge City has a new school house," says Kitty. "What is it Kitty,' asks Matt. "Matt, the letter is from Ben and Elizabeth, signing over all their property to the people of Dodge City!" "Well, I sure would like to see Garth Brakus' face when he hears about this," says Doc. Festus says, "I think I'll go over yonder an tell him my ownself!" "I think this calls for a toast to the one that got away," sys Kitty. "I shore wish I could drink ta that!" Festus is at the bar with an empty glass: "Sam!"(Kitty). Sure Miss Kitty, here Festus," says Sam. "Much obliged Sam, Miss Kitty!"(Festus)

Is. 60.21: Your people shall be righteous; they shall possess the land forever, the shoot of my planting, the work of my hands, that I might be glorified.

Is. 40.31: But they who wait for the Lord shall renew their strength, they shall mount up with wings like eagles, they shall run and not be weary, they shall walk and not faint.

Prov. 18.16: A man's gift makes room for him and brings him before great men.

2. Ex-Convict, Phoenix[51]: Festus encounters an ex-convict on the boardwalk in front of the Marshal's office: **"Morn'n! Yer name Phoenix is it?"** "That's right," says Phoenix **"I'm Festus Haggen. I'm the Deputy Marshal here in Dodge."** "I reckon you didn't burn my 'Wanted' picture," Phoenix replies. **"Well, I'm think'n yer ah mean'n Marshal Dillon an not me, he shore did burn it! Now I ain't gonna bother ya none, but I'll be fix'n ta ask ya ah couple questions."** "Like what?" **"You was in Leavenworth wasn't ya?"** "That's right!" **"Well, I jist got word that ah feller escaped from up yonder an I thought you might ah run across't him."** "What's his name?" **"Sontag! John Sontag! You know'd him did ya?"** "Nope!" **"Are ya shore?"** "I'm sure!" **"Well OK then, but if'n ya change yer mind on recollect'n**

---
51 1971-72: Season 17, Series No. 541, No. 2 in season, written by Anthony Lawrence.

him, be shore ta let me an the Marshal know right pronto like!" "I won't be staying in Kansas that long. I'm head'n to California!" "Oh now, yer make'n tracks are ya?" "You might just say I'm moving on west and starting a new life!"

Ps. 79.11: Let the groans of the prisoners come before thee; according to thy great power preserve those doomed to die!

Ps. 102.20: To hear the groans of the prisoners, to set free those who were doomed to die.

Ps. 107.10-11: Some sat in darkness and in gloom, prisoners in affliction and in irons, for they had rebelled against the words of God, and spurned the counsel of the Most High.

Jn. 8.32: "And you will know the truth, and the truth will make you free."

---

3. Miss Tara[52]**:** Festus finds Newly outside the barn where the town square dance is being held. He interrupts Newly while he is just about to kiss Tara, his girl friend. **"Oh! Howdy Newly, there ya be! I been ah look'n everplace fer ya. Well, hello Miss Tara! Newly, I'm awful sorry ta intrude on ya like this here, but Mathew has more prisoners than he can handle by his ownself, so I'm fix'n ta ride up ta Mankato**

---
[52] 1971-72: Season 17, Series No. 557, No. 18 in season, written by Wm. Kelley.

with him, mean'n that yer in charge! Beg'n yer pardon Miss Tara! Start'n right now! All right?" "You bet Festus," says Newly. "Oops, wait jist ah minute, here's yer badge all polished up fer ya!" "OK, you and Matt just take it easy Festus." Festus says, "You jist brought up the onlyest two gaits Ruth's got, slow and easy! Heh..heh...heh!"

Prov. 18.18-19: The lot puts an end to disputes and decides between powerful contenders. A brother helped is like a strong city, but quarreling is like the bars of a castle.

---

4. Miss Phoebe[53]: "Good morn'n Miss Phoebe!" "Good morning Festus, just what are you doing out here?" "Well, I have me some papers ta serve fer Mathew!" "O, clear out here at this hour?" "Sure as yer born! I'm out here an all, an if there is anything I could hep ya with I'd be tickled ta hep ya!" "Oh, no, no I don't need any help thank you." "Yes em!" "I'd invite you in for coffee, but..." "Oh no, Oh no that's all right Miss Phoebe, I'll jist head on back to Dodge."

Prov. 25.13: Like the cold of snow in the time of harvest is a faithful messenger to those who send him, he refreshes the spirit of his masters.

---

[53] 1971-72: Season 17, Series No. 561, No. 22 in season, written by Ron Honthaner.

5. Festus, Square Dance Caller[54]**:** Festus is calling the barn square dance in Dodge: **"Grab yer partner, bow ta yer waist, wave yer hands, grab yer hands circle go round, drop yer hands, change yer circle, swing yer arms, skip to-da-do, grab yer partner, swing her on home, round an round, hands ta the right, four by four, grab yer hands and twirl round, change yer hands and circle round, females now grab yer hands three by three, circle round, doe-see-doe, allemande left round ya go! Whew! We'll take a rest fer ah spell folks!"**

Prov. 10.20: The tongue of the righteous is choice silver; the mind of the wicked is of little worth.

Prov. 8.2-3: On heights beside the way, in paths she takes her stand; beside the gates in front of the town, at the entrance of the portals she cries aloud.

―❦―

"Mathew when ya git back to Dodge, don't tell ole Doc that I'm ah coming back in ta town too quick so as he can enjoy his-self fer ah few days!" "Festus, Doc won't be fit to live with till you get back to Dodge, you know that," says Matt. "Well fiddle, I know that Mathew, and ole Doc knows it too, but if he know'd that I know'd he know'd, why he'd turn seven ways of purple and deny it. See ya directly Matthew."

---

54 1971-72: Season 17, Series No. 557, No. 18 in season, written by Wm. Kelley.

Prov. 18.24: There are friends who pretend to be friends, but there is a friend who sticks closer than a brother.

Prov. 17.17: A friend loves at all times, and a brother is born for adversity.

Prov. 27.6: Faithful are the wounds of a friend; profuse are the kisses of an enemy.

---

6. Festus Speaks Mexican[55]: Festus claims he can speak Mexican: **"Well, 'cause I talk Mexicans, and I would had me an understand'n with them folks before ya could say, 'a rat went over a roof with a piece of raw liver in its mouth'!"** "Well say something in Mexicans then," says Doc. **"Me sombrero is roacho." "My sombrero is red? Now that's really helpful Festus! You'd be standing there with your red hat in your hand while Matt's getting himself beat to a pulp! And I suppose that you probably can very fluently carry two or three words!"** Kitty speaks a long eloquent sentence to Festus in Spanish: **Festus asks, "What's that mean Miss Kitty?" "It means, if you don't keep quiet and drink your beer, I'm going to throw you out of here before I count to three!" "Now that's the best idea I've heard yet! And if you can silencio, I'll buy the next round! Is that a fair deal Matt?"(Doc). That's**

---

55 19767-768: Season 13, Series No. 460, No. 22 in season, written by Calvin Clements, Jr.

fair enough, don't you think so Festus?"(Matt). Festus says, "Se, muchous grouchious Doc, you ornery ole scudder you!"

Ecc. 3.1,7: For everything there is a season, and a time for every matter under heaven: a time to rend and a time to sew; a time to keep silence, and a time to speak.

Job 11.2-3: "Should a multitude of words go unanswered; and a man full of talk be vindicated? Should your babble silence men, and when you mock, shall no one shame you?"

1Cor. 12.10: To another the working of miracles, to another prophecy, to another the ability to distinguish between spirits, to another various kinds of tongues, to another the interpretation of tongues.

---

7. Festus' Baby Prediction[57]: "What do you mean you can tell what a baby is going to be, a boy or a girl before it is born," asks Doc. "Now the way ya can tell what the baby is go'n to be, is ya tie a long string to her wedding band and hold it like ah 'pendolium' over her belly, and if it swings clockerwise it's ah girl, if it swings contrary clockerwise it's ah boy. Now if it swings neither way, but jist back and forth, it's GAS!"

---

57 1968-69: Season 14, Series No. 483, No. 20 in season, written by Jack Hawn.

Prov. 20.11: Even a child makes himself known by his acts, whether what he does is pure and right.

Ecc. 3.1-2: For everything there is a season, and a time for every matter under heaven: A time to be born, and a time to die.

---

8. Learn to Read & Write[58]: "Why don't you learn to read and write," asks Doc. "Supose'n I was to go to work and learn how to read write'n, well how do I know that the feller that wrote the write'n was write'n the write'n right? It could be he wrote the write'n all wrong and here'd I'd be read'n the write'n all wrong! Don't ya see?"

Prov. 8.5: O simple ones, learn prudence; O foolish man, pay attention.

Prov. 18.15: An intelligent mind acquires knowledge, and the ear of the wise seeks knowledge.

---

9. Deadly Mistaken Identity[59]: Festus and Doc are walking down the boardwalk talking about how and who should

---

[58] Various episodes with Festus Haggen from Season 12, 1966-67 through Season 20, 1974-75
[59] 1971-72: Season 17, Series No. 562, No. 23 in season, written by Calvin Clements, Sr.

be taking care of the sick when doctors are done with them: "Who's gonna take care of folks then Doc? Some people can make do on their own, don't ya see?" "That don't mean we don't need a hospital in Dodge," says Doc. Festus says, "Now wait ah minute now! I'll tell ya jist what'll hap'n if we was ta git ah hospital in Dodge! You'd need somebody ta be set'n up with folks all night, don't ya see Doc?" "Yes I do, and that's exactly what they need and that's causing these gray hairs of mine!"

A government law agent of the Indian Territory (Doyle) and a witness to a crime (Raines) are watching Festus and Doc: "**Is that the one?**" Doyle shows a photo of Festus' likeness to Raines: "**Are you sure that's the one? I want to be absolutely sure about this,**" says Doyle. "Yes, that's him! Do they have the fellow in the picture in jail here in Dodge," asks Raines. Doyle says, "I want positive identification!" "That's him!"(Raines). "Not the slightest doubt in your mind?"(Doyle). "NO!" (Raines). "Well here he comes. I'll handle it! YOU'RE under arrest mister and I'll take that firearm!"(Doyle). Festus yells out, "What in tarnation!" "I said put your hands behind your back! Get up on your feet!"(Doyle). "HERE, HERE, QUIT THAT! What do you think you're doing! Put that gun down," says Doc.

Matt comes out of his office to see what is going on and says, "What's this all about?" "Official work of the government! I'm the Marshal of Indian Territory, and I'm placing this man under arrest! I have a warrant," Doyle says. Matt tells him, "The first thing you've got to do is learn how to serve it! What's the charge," asks Matt. "Three counts of murder lodged against one Frank Eaton for starters," says Doyle, and Festus yells out, "I ain't no Frank Eaton!" "His name is Festus Haggen," says Doc. "Yeah, one of his many aliases! No matter what name he goes by now, this is the man I'm after!"(Doyle)

Doyle shows a picture of Festus' likeness, and another picture of Festus from long ago sitting on a RR track eating lunch: **"Who's identifying him,"** Matt asks. **"I've only seen him once and was only briefly so I had a corroborating witness brought in with me,"** says Doyle. **"That's me Marshal,"** says Raines. **"Why I ain't never saw you in my whole life, and you neither,"** says Festus. **"You're just mistaken,"** says Doc. **"He lined up the four of us and started shooting! I'm just lucky to be alive, the others weren't! When a man shoots off your arm from a distance of ten feet, you're not about to forget his face or his name,"** Raines yells out.

Jer. 8.18 My grief is beyond healing, my heart is sick within me.

Prov. 13.12: Hope deferred makes the heart sick, but a desire fulfilled is a tree of life.

Ps. 119.29: Put false ways far from me; and graciously teach me thy law!

Ps.119.104: Through thy precepts I get understanding; therefore I hate every false way.

Ps. 119.163: I hate and abhor falsehood, but I love thy law.

Festus, Matt, Doc, Doyle, and Raines appeared before Ford County Circuit Judge Clayborn and after an agonizing and perplexing conversation and no proof to the contrary, Festus was arraigned on suspicion of murder on the word of eye witness Mr. Raines, and sent to the jail in nearby Rock Creek in Indian Territory to face trial for murder and armed robbery.

Prov. 30.8: Remove far from me falsehood and lying; give me neither poverty nor riches; feed me with the food that is needful for me.

Ex. 20.16: "You shall not bear false witness against your neighbor."

Prov. 14.5: A faithful witness does not lie, but a false witness breathes out lies.

Prov. 14.25: A truthful witness saves lives, but one who utters lies is a betrayer.

Prov. 24.28-29: Be not a witness against your neighbor without cause, and do not deceive with your lips. Do not say, "I will do to him as he has done to me; I will pay the man back for what he has done."

Prov. 25.18: A man who bears false witness against his neighbor is like a war club, or a sword, or a sharp arrow.

Festus slowly handed his gun to Newly and respectfully removed his badge and handed it to the Judge. The Judge looked on with a forlorn and sympathetic expression.

Ps. 107.10: Some sat in darkness and in gloom, prisoners in affliction and in irons.

Jn. 16.32: "The hour is coming, indeed it has come, when you will be scattered, every man to his home, and will leave me alone; yet I am not alone, for the Father is with me."

Tit. 1.16: They profess to know God, but they deny him by their deeds; they are detestable, disobedient, unfit for any good deed.

2Peter 2.1: But false prophets also arose among the people, just as there will be false teachers among you, who will secretly bring in destructive heresies, even denying the Master who brought them, bringing upon themselves swift destruction.

Job 18.17: "His memory perishes from the earth, and he has no name in the street."

⁓

Matt tracked down the real Frank Eaton through his brother and his wife Susie Johnson who earlier testified against Festus by claiming he was her husband Frank Eaton that she claimed was dead. The trial was over and Festus was sentenced to hang on Monday at noon.

Prov. 10.7: The memory of the righteous is a blessing, but the name of the wicked will rot.

Ps. 119.21: Thou dost rebuke the insolent, accursed ones, who wander from thy commandments.

Is. 46.8: Remember this and consider, recall it to mind, you transgressors.

Ezek. 20.43: And there you shall remember your ways and all the doings with which you have polluted yourselves; and you shall loathe yourselves for all the evils that you have committed.

Lev. 5.4: Or if anyone utters with his lips a rash oath, to do evil or to do good, any sort of rash oath that men swear, and it is hidden from him, when he comes to know it he shall in any of these be guilty.

2Peter 2.9: Then the Lord knows how to rescue the godly from trial, and to keep the unrighteous under punishment until the day of judgment.

Is. 10.3: What will you do on the day of punishment, in the storm that will come from afar? To whom will you flee for help, and where will you leave your wealth?

Lam. 3.52: "I have been hunted like a bird by those who were my enemies without cause; they flung me alive into the pit and cast stones on me."

Hos. 4.3: Therefore the land mourns, and all who dwell in it languish, and also the beasts of the field, and the birds of the air; and even the fish of the sea are taken away.

The stagecoach stopped at Owl Head Station and among the passengers that got off to stretch their legs was Matt. Susie Johnson was there to meet the stage and tended to the passengers and horses: **"Well hello Mrs. Eaton! You'll be glad to know that we got a stay of execution by the Governor for your husband!"(Matt). "That's, ….that's real fine." (Susie Johnson). "Also a retrial, and it's going to be held in Adelia Springs!"(Matt)**

Matt saw a familiar white horse tied to a post on the side of a shed, and he recognized it belonging to Burk, Dodge

City's freight office clerk for the Adams Freight Co.: "We're moving out Marshal!"(Stage Driver). "It's real good news Marshal, about Frank getting a new trial and all!" (Susie Johnson)

2Chr. 20:22: And when they began to sing and praise, the Lord set an ambush against the men of Ammon, Moab, and Mount Seir, who had come against Judah, so that they were routed.

Josh. 8.9: So Joshua sent them forth; and they went to the place of ambush, and lay between Bethel and Ai, to the west of Ai; but Joshua spent that night among the people.

The stage pulled out of Owl Head Station with Matt on it, but he halted the stage when it rounded a bend and was hidden from sight by a grove of trees. Matt got off the stage and on foot he quietly doubled back to Owl Head Station: **"Susie, who was that man you were talking to out there?"(Eaton). "It was Dodge's Marshal. There's going to be a new trial he says!"(Susie Johnson). "Lucky man! A bullet is a lot better than a rope once the Marshal gets out of hearing range!"(Eaton).** Susie looks out the window and sees that the stage is gone and out of sight: **"They're out of sight Frank!"(Susie)**

Ps. 69.14: Hide not thy face from thy servant; for I am in distress, make haste to answer me.

Prov. 24.11: Rescue those who are being taken away to death; hold back those who are stumbling to the slaughter.

―❦―

Meanwhile Matt made his way back to the station Newly and Doyle rode to meet the stage and to tell Matt that Festus broke jail to avoid being hung by an angry mob, They met the stage down the road. They inquired about Matt and learned that he got off the stage a couple of miles back. Back at the station Festus was there and about to be shot, but in an act of desperation, he flipped the table up in front of Eaton and broke away, and Eaton fired and wounded him as he tried to escape across the station yard. Matt appeared from behind the corner of the station shed and shot Eaton. He was dead where he fell as Newly and Doyle rode in: **"Festus! You all right?"(Matt). "Jist grazed Mathew! Well Newly she's all over!"(Festus). "Doyle, there's your Frank Eaton!"(Matt). "Not much to say is there? I'll get that woman for you Marshal. You take care of your friend Festus!"(Doyle)**

So, Festus was gone for quite a spell and suffered a close brush with the gallows due to a mistaken identity. His friends defended him to no avail, but Matt rescued him and caught the real Frank Eaton. Festus missed his birthday celebration with his friends, but he was back in Dodge City and he was given a surprise birthday party and cake in the Long Branch Saloon. All his friends were there, Kitty, Matt, Newly, Doc, and all the town folks. Doc was sitting across the table from Festus: **"Golly be I jist don't know what all ta say about this here cake an party!"(Festus). "Well don't say anything then!"(Doc). "How old are you Festus?"(Matt). "Well let me see, it was about the same time that momma's ole sow had that big litter of pigs!"(Festus). "What a way to remember a birthday. Good heavens let's get started, my mouth has been watering ever since I saw Kitty put those strawberries and that merangy stuff on that cake, blow them candles out and let's get started!"(Doc). "Make a wish first Festus!"(Kitty). "Well let me see, oh ya here goes!! Pfffffffftt!!"(Festus). The merangy stuff got all over Doc's face and he said, "HE's BACK!"**

Ps. 116.7: Return, O my soul, to your rest; for the Lord has dealt bountifully with you.

Prov. 14.32: The wicked is overthrown through his evil doing, but the righteous finds refuge through his integrity.

Jn. 15.13: "Greater love has no man than this, that a man lay down his life for his friends."

10. Rope of Snakes[60]: In the Long Branch, Festus is attempting to tell a story, but keeps getting interrupted by Doc, Matt, and Newly: "Festus, I'll tell you if Newly had told me that story, I'd believe every word of it," says Matt. "It's the Gospel truth now! If I'm ah lie'n, I'm ah die'n! But that ain't noth'n near so hard to believe as what happened to me ah few years back. I was trapp'n mushrats down in the Sustaroo Swamp, and all of ah sudden there I was clean up to my armpits in quickie sand with circled clean round me was watery 'mosicins' ah snapp'n at my vitals." An interruption occurs when Doc comes in and sits down and starts talking, but Festus continues to tell his tale: "and anyhow I grabbed ah hold this first snake and I pinched his jaws tagether like that don't ya see? And I made him glom on ta that next snake's tail!"

An interruption occurs again by Doc talking: "Now wait ah minute Doc, I'm jist git'n to the interest'n part, don't ya want ta hear the rest of my story?" "No! I'm tired, and I'm going up to my office and take a long nap!"... "There ya go ah'gin with ah thimble full of silly words stringed ta'gether so they don't mean ah blamed thing.....Anyhow, Doc, these here watery 'mosicins' was ah move'n in fer the kill"...Doc gets up to walk out and Festus continues: "but do ya think I's scared? Pffftt! I'll tell ya Doc what ya got ta say ain't near as interest'n as snakes is. So long to ya Doc....

---

60 Various conversations by Festus Haggen from Season 12: 1966-67 through Season 20, 1974-75.

Well, let's see where was I?" "You were just getting ready to tie the snakes together to make a rope out of them to pull yourself out of the swamp," says Newly. "Oh! Ya hear'd it before did ya?"

"Now I'll tell ya someth'n, it wasn't as easy as all that. Ya know with them watery 'mosicins' ah be'n so slipperty attaway, every time I was to go to work an tie ah knot in em then they would slip loose, don't ya see? So I'll tell ya what I'd ta done. I retched in there and I got me ah handful of that quickie sand, squorshed the water out of it, then I sanded them watery 'mosicins' down, and that'a way I could pull my ownself out with them there snakes like ah rope, don't ya see?"

Job 11.2-3: "Should a multitude of words go unanswered; and a man full of talk be vindicated? Should your babble silence men, and when you mock, shall no one shame you?"

Ps. 40.2: He drew me up from the desolate pit, out of the miry bog, and set my feet upon a rock, making my steps secure.

Lk. 24.11: But these words seemed to them an idle tale, and they did not believe them.

11. Surprise Gunfight in Dodge[61]: Matt asks Festus how the gunfight got started: **"Them three scraggyests was ah fix'n to cause a heap ah trouble. Well I was ah come'n out of the freight office and I see'd these three fellers stand'n out there in the street all spraddled out an ah badger'n this here feller that jist got off the stage. Now when I see'd this here Deek Tower, I figured we had us ah hold the wrong end of the rope, but this one feller that was ah git'n off'n the stage, he jist fired off an knocked him kick'n along with those two other fellers, Buck Leonard an Sundog Wheeler, and he never even broke his eye-balls ah do'n it. All three of em Mathew! They's the worst look'n ever there was. I don't know why they did it, but those fellers weren't exactly friends. Mathew, this here fella did everything he could ta talk his self out'a that scrape, but they wouldn't listen at him. Now I didn't try to hold him over, 'cause it was the champeendy'ist case of self defense that I'd ever saw!"**

Prov. 1.17-19: For in vain is a net spread in the sight of any bird; but these men lie in wait for their own blood, they set an ambush for their own lives. Such are the ways of all who get gain by violence; it takes away the life of its possessors.

---

[61] 1973-74: Season 19, Series No. 592, No. 5 in season, written by Paul F. Edwards.

12. A Quiet Day in Dodge[62]: Matt is exhausted after being without sleep for 36 hours and is trying to get some sleep on a cot in his office, and along comes Festus who is returning from fishing. He is singing while walking down main street with a gunny bag full of catfish, and he's heading for the office and comes into the office talking loudly and making all matter of noise: **"FISH, big catfish wait'n ta be et, FISH, big catfish wait'n ta be et! FISH big catfish, FISH big catfish by my dog tracks, fry me some bacon grease, catfish in ah pan, fry me some taters in ah little fat, boil me some coffee along with all that, an warsh er all down with hot coffee! Pffurr, pffurr, pffurr!"**

Matt just dozed off: **"MATHEW!" "What is it Festus?" "When'd you git back?"** "About five minutes ago." **"Where ya been at the last couple ah days? We got fret'n about ya!"** "I've been trailing Joe Snelling." **"JOE SNELLING? Where'd ya run acrosst him at?"** "FESTUS! I'll tell you about it later. Right now I have to sleep. I have been up 36 hours!" **"Course, you go ahead an git yerself some sleep! Ya blame shore need it!"**

Festus empties his gunnysack full of catfish on the lunch table with all sorts of clattery banging, his shoes scraping on the floor and spurs jingling while Matt is trying to go back to sleep: **"MATHEW? MATHEW? You asleep yet?"** "What is it Festus?" **"Did ya git Snelling?"** "Yes, I got him. He's in the back." **"You go ahead on back ta sleep! You shore blame need it if anybody does!"** (Clatter bang, clatter, stomp, jingle, scrape, thump). **"FESTUS!" "What is it Mathew?"**

---

62 1972-73: Season 18, Series No. 582, No. 19 in season, written by Jack Miller.

Festus walks over to Matt while holding two large catfish by their tails in front of Matt's face: **"GET THAT OUTA HERE!"** "Git what?" "You going to clean those fish here?" "Well course Mathew! Catfish got'a be cleaned quick else wise they're liable to sour on ya! Anybody knows that!" "Can't you take them outside and do it out there?" "OH! That's ah good idea Mathew! I'll do that!"

With all manner of noise, Festus starts dragging the table across the floor to the door and attempts to take the table through the door opening; Jingle, clattery, clack, scrape, scratch, clatter, bang, and finally gets through the door which he slams with a bang. Then he comes back into the office: **"Mathew? What er ya fix'n ta do with Snelling?"** "Take him over to Judge Brooker this afternoon after I get some sleep!" "OH!"

He drags a chair across the floor to the doorway, and opens door with a bang against the wall and picks up the catfish that fell scattered all over the floor. He finally gets back out the door with a bang, then comes back in the office with another slam of the door: **"OH! MATHEW? I forgot ta tell ya! Judge Brooker? He ain't gonna be here later on taday! I hear'd him say he's fix'n ta take that half-past-six stage up ta Hays! So if yer fix'n ta see him it better be moocho pronto!"** "Uh, huh! Maybe I'll get a little sleep in a few minutes." It is 5:30 a.m.: "Yeah! Goodnight Mathew!" **"FESTUS! Wake me up at a quarter to six will you?"** "You betcha! I'm gonna fix ya the best catfish breakfast that ya ever slapped ah lip on! I guarantee ya!" Stomp, stomp, jingle, jingle, scrape, scrape, and the door opens and slams shut and Festus, while whistling and singing, goes to work cleaning his catfish out in front of the office on the boardwalk, while Matt struggles to go to sleep.

Ecc. 4.6: Better is a handful of quietness than two hands full of toil and a striving after the wind.

Job 34.29: "When he is quiet, who can condemn? When he hides his face, who can behold him, whether it be a nation or a man?"

Is. 32.18: My people will abide in a peaceful habitation, in secure dwellings, and in quiet resting places.

---

13. A Hot Day in Dodge[63]: Festus is having lunch at Delmonico's when he sees Doc walking down the street from the blacksmith shop, so he leaves the table and takes off across the street to run into Doc to tell him he'll buy him a beer down at the Long Branch. A conversation ensues between them: **"Doc! Whew! She's hotter'n ah jug full of red ants ain't she?" "NO!"(Doc) "NO?" "NO! I won't buy you a beer!"(Doc) "Well if that ain't the down rightedness orneriest thing I ever,,, I didn't ask ya to!" "I knew you were going to though! I knew exactly what you were going to say!" "I wasn't go'n ta do no such thing! Fact is I was fix'n ta offer ta buy ya a beer!" "Ha, Ha, of course you were! Your**

---
63 1972-73: Season 18, Series No. 583, No. 20 in season, written by Ron Bishop.

According to Festus

pockets are always bulging with money!" "All right Mr. Smart Alec, what's that look like to ya. That right there!"

Festus flashes a silver dollar in Doc's face: "Now where'd you get that?" "I been work'n!" "Now I asked you a simple question and there's no reason to lie to me Festus!" "I aint't story'n to ya now Doc! I went ta work an put new shoes on six old man Scrog's horses an he give me that dollar!" (Festus flips a silver dollar in the air).

"Ha! Now you are just going out and squander it on something foolish! Why don't you take that money and invest it in something! Why don't you do that?"(Doc). "Invest in WHAT?"(Festus). "There are wonderful land values outside of Dodge! Now why don't you go out there someplace, look around and buy yourself a lot?"(Doc). "A lot of what?"(Festus). A LOT! A Lot of land!"(Doc). "Oh fiddle, I can't afford ta buy ah lot ah land! Ya prob'ly could, the way ya been bilk'n and gouge'n folks!"(Festus). "Oh, hush up! I'm trying to help you for heaven's sake! It don't cost a whole lot to buy a little lot!"(Doc). "What'd ya mean? It don't cost ah whole lot ta buy ah little lot? Er... or ah whole lot ta buy ah lot? What'd ya mean?"(Festus). "I mean a little lot of land!" (Doc). "There ain't no such thing! Ah little's ah little and ah lots ah lot! There ain't no little lot, or ah lot ah little! Don't ya see? Now ya want that beer or don't ya?"(Festus). "NO! I'm all worn out!"(Doc)

Doc walks away exhausted: **"If ya change yer mind, me an Newly will be over to the Long Branch have'n ah whole lot of little beers! Pffft! I'm buy'n!"**

Ps. 37.11: But the meek shall possess the land, and delight themselves in abundant prosperity.

Heb. 13.5-6: Keep your life free from love of money, and be content with what you have; for he has said, "I will never fail you nor forsake you."

---

14. It's Scary[64]: "It's scary! Don't ya hear it Doc? It ain't been this quiet in Dodge since Heck was ah pup." "How do you hear quiet?" "Well Doc all ya got'a do is listen at it. If'n ya don't hear noth'n then yer hear'n quiet, don't ya see? It's jist blame quiet! I been hear'n it all night long. Noth'n but thundersome quiet, it's jist plain spooky. Let me tell ya there's someth'n fix'n ta happen and when she busts loose it's go'n to be ah two-toed turkey tatted too-baloo and ya can mark my word on that!"

Ecc. 4.6: Better is a handful of quietness than two hands full of toil and a striving after the wind.

Ecc. 9.17: The words of the wise heard in quiet are better than the shouting of a ruler among fools.

---

64 1972-73: Season 18, Series No. 578, No. 15 in season, written by Dudley Bromley.

Ezek. 3.27: "But when I speak with you, I will open your mouth, and you shall say to them, 'Thus says the Lord God'; he that will hear, let him hear; and he that will refuse to hear, let him refuse; for they are a rebellious house."

---

15. Doc's Pain Pills[65]**:** Doc comes around the corner from his office and runs into Festus: **"Why don't you look where you're going!"**(Doc) **"Yer like ah blamed ole wall eyed buffalo in ah hen house!"**(Festus). **"Where you been anyway?"**(Doc). **"Busy!"**(Festus). **"Busy? You were supposed to let me look at those ribs!"**(Doc). **"Ya done had yer last look at them ribs, ya clammy handed ole quack!"**(Festus). **"Well that's just fine. I'll send you my bill!"**(Doc). **"BILL! Well ya done got all the money in Ford county, how much more do ya want?"**(Festus). **"Just what I've earned, that's all!"**(Doc). **"Earned my foot, ah pok'n, ah prodd'n, an ah pound'n them little ole pain pills, ya'd orta be throwd in jail!"**(Festus)

Rom. 4.4: Now to one who works, his wages are not reckoned as a gift but as his due.

---

16. A Cold Draft[66]**:** Doc is giving Festus a tetanus shot in his rear-end: **"This is not going to hurt a bit!"**(Doc) **"Oh, I ain't ah frett'n about yer blamed needle, I'm frett'n about**

---

65 Various conversations by Festus Haggen from Season 12: 1966-67 through Season 20, 1974-75.
66 Ibid.

that there cold draft on that there behind'n me! Shut that dang door Burk! Doc, I'm go'n ta pinch that pinhead of his plum off one of these days! Ya reckon ya fellers could do yer blabber'n after my britches is got up? I'm fix'n to knock knots on Burk's head faster'n he can rub em!"

Prov. 16.18: Pride goes before a fall, and a haughty spirit before a fall.

---

17. Doc's Escort[67]: Festus is taking Doc to see some hill-county folks for a doctor call: **"You sure you know where you're going Festus?"(Doc) "Well of course I do Doc! Onlyest folks I hear'd about is jist over that pass. I'll tell ya someth'n else I hear'd, they ain't too friendlyest ah bunch." "You mean they are outlaws?" "No not that Doc, they jist like to stay by their ownselves!"(Festus)**

Is. 2.10: Enter into the rock and hide in the dust from before the terror of the Lord, and from the glory of his majesty.

Is. 32.2: Each will be like a hiding place from the wind, a covert from the tempest, like streams of water in a dry place, like the shade of a great rock in a weary land.

---

67 1973-74: Season 19, Series No. 598, No. 11 in season, written by Calvin Clements, Sr.

18. Dr. Newly[68]: "Newly, ya hadn't orta be squaller'n at these folks like that. Now I know they roughed ya up ah good deal, but it ain't go'n to be easy fer ya, but yer go'n have ta learn how ta talk ta these folks. See, they'ns got theys own way ah do'n things, and of course ya figger'd ya know the way things orta be did. Maybe yer both ah little bit right. They jist people, men, women, an young'ns an such as that. Don't ya see?"

Prov. 17.10: A rebuke goes deeper into a man of understanding than a hundred blows into a fool.

---

19. Festus' Ague[69]: Newly meets Festus on the street and hears him moaning and groaning: "What's the trouble Festus," asks Newly. "Oh Newly, it's them blamed argues, they's ah come'n on me again!" "Well have you been taking that medicine Doc gave you?" "Of course....well, fact is NO! I ain't an I'll tell ya why. Ya know that stuff he mixed-up smells like someth'n he brewed up in ah fit'd cat's nest!" Doc comes on the scene: "I don't want to talk to you," says Doc. "Well who's asked ta talk ta ya?" "I distinctly told you that I didn't want to hear any complaints until you finished that medicine bottle!"(Doc) "Well it's done finished!"(Festus). "Finished? Yes it's finished....poured

---

68 1973-74: Season 19, Series No. 598, No. 11 in season, written by Calvin Clements, Sr.
69 Various conversations by Festus Haggen from Season 12: 1966-67 through Season 20, 1974-75.

out on the ground, and don't tell me you didn't do it, because somebody saw you pour it out!"(Doc). "All right nosey, I'll tell ya what I done, I poured that blamed concocteration out by ah prairie dog hole, not in it, but beside it, an directly come that ole prairie dog jist ah sputter'n an ah choke'n and pertineye keeled over dead, and that there was down wind, an that's ah pure o'lee fact!"(Festus)

Job 7.11: "Therefore I will not restrain my mouth; I will speak in the anguish of my spirit; I will complain in the bitterness of my soul."

Job 23.2: "Today also my complaint is bitter, his hand is heavy in spite of my groaning."

Ps. 55.17: Evening and morning and at noon I utter my complaint and moan, and he will hear my voice.

---

20. Smokey Hill Country[70]: "Ya fix'n ta go after em are ya Mathew?" "Yes I am Festus." "Well ya ain't ah go'n all by yer ownself are ya," Festus asks. "That's exactly what I'm going to do and I want you to stay here and look after things."(Matt). "Well now Mathew, I know that Smokey Hill River country better'n ah baby knows his momma, and them Sutterfields they's ah hair trigger'n outfit jist

---

[70] 1973-74: Season 19, Series No. 588-89, No. 1&2 in season, written by Jim Byrnes.

meaner'n ah four headed rattlesnake. Now yer liable to need me!"

Prov. 28.4: Those who forsake the law praise the wicked, but those who keep the law strive against them.

Prov. 29.18: Where there is no prophecy the people cast off restraint, but blessed is he who keeps the law.

—⁂—

"Why don't you take Festus with you when you go after those outlaws Matt," asks Kitty. "I think that's a great idea Matt. Why don't you do that, take Festus with you and then we can all get a little peace and quiet around here," says Doc. Festus retorts, "All right ya blamed ole scudder, if I was ta ever leave Dodge ya'd be miserabler'n a flea bit ole hound dog with a rhumeeticky hind leg, besides that ya wouldn't find nobody that would put up with yer blamed ole pickety-picken upon!"

Job 16.2-3: "I have heard many such things; miserable comforters are you all. Shall windy words have an end? Or what provokes you that you answer?"

—⁂—

21. Reclaiming Hilt[71]: Matt, Newly, and Festus enter the town of Hilt to reclaim the town from killers who are raising havoc with the town folks. Festus comes up to the ringleader who is playing poker and blowing his tater-trap and walks up to him at a poker table: **"Yer name Badger is it?"(Festus). "Ya, who wants to know?"(Badger). "There's ah big feller out yonder with ah Marshal's badge pinned on his shirt. He told me ta tell ya someth'n." "He did?"(Badger). "Either ya come out yonder er he's fix'n ta come in here an git ya. If I was ya I wouldn't settle down here fer the night, it appears ta me he meant business!"**

Job 15.35: "They conceive mischief and bring forth evil and their heart prepares deceit."

Lam. 4.18-19: "Men dogged our steps so that we could not walk in our streets; our end drew near; our days were numbered for our end had come."

---

22. Old Nag[72]: **"What's the matter with that old nag you got there Festus,"** Doc asks. **"Well Doc don't ya see, a horse can't be ah pull'n whilst he's ah kick'n and that's ah fact I'm mention'n, and he can't kick whilst he's ah pull'n, and that's my contention-someness. I'm think'n of initiate'n**

---

71 1973-74: Season 19, Series No. 604, No. 17 in season, written by Paul Savage.
72 Various conversations by Festus Haggen from Season 12: 1966-67 through Season 20, 1974-75.

that ole horse ta lead his-self ah life that's more an fitt'n and have him pull an honest-someness load, an then there'll be no time fer him to be ah kick'n. Don't ya see?"

Job 12.12: "Wisdom is with the aged, and understanding in length of days."

Job 15.10: "Both the gray-haired and the aged are among us, older than your father."

---

23. Bad Apples[73]: "I seen him! He jist rode in plain as ah burro on ah skyline," says Festus. "Who's that," Matt asks. "Talley! That wickeder'n a rattler feller Talley, that's who!" "I thought he was up in Ellsworth!"(Matt). "NO! He's where the money is, and the money is where the trouble is, and see'n he's here it sure is wings to a bird that they's trouble around someplace!" "Was he alone?"(Matt). "NO, it's his wife and daughter with him, it appeared like!" "Now Festus, that doesn't hardly sound like a hunting party now does it?"(Matt). "But Mathew I don't give ah hoot if he rode into town on ah wagon load of Bibles, ya know'd what his reputation is. Ya know what I mean Mathew? Bad apples!"

---

[73] 1973-74: Season 19, Series No. 606, No. 19 in season, written by Ron Bishop.

Prov. 2.2: Making your ear attentive to wisdom and inclining your heart to understanding.

Prov. 10.30: The righteous will never be removed, but the wicked will not dwell in the land.

Prov. 16.4: The Lord has made everything for its purpose, even the wicked for the day of trouble.

---

24. Kitty's Orphan Baby[74]: Kitty is taken with an orphan baby that Matt found in a cave with a young girl. She decided to keep the baby, much to Doc's and everyone's concern: Kitty was buying baby clothes for the child at the dry goods store when Festus came along: **"All right Festus, you can put her in the carriage now,"** Kitty says. "Heh, heh, ya little bitty ole scudder, you ain't no bigger'n a tater bud. Beetie, beetie, bottie…bottie, bottie, beetie!"(Festus). "What are you doing with that baby," asks Doc. "Why don't ya let ah feller know yer around? Ya come ah slip'n up like ah blamed ole coyote through ah fence bolt!"(Festus). "What are you doing to that baby?"(Doc). "Well I'm make'n her laugh!" "Making her laugh, with an ugly face full of whiskers like that? You're scare'n her to death!" "Now ya jist hold on!"(Festus). "Where'd you get the buggy?"(Doc) "Miss

---

[74] 1973-74: Season 19, Series No. 605, No. 18 in season, written by Jim Byrnes.

Kitty jist blamed bought it fer her!"(Festus). "Where's Miss Kitty?"(Doc)."Back yonder there in the store ... Pffttt!"(Festus). With much anguish, Kitty reluctantly gave the orphan baby to a widow who lost her only child a few years back.

Mk. 10.13-14: And they were bringing children to him, that he might touch them; and the disciples rebuked them. But when Jesus saw it he was indignant, and said to them, "Let the children come to me, do not hinder them; for to such belongs the kingdom of God.

---

25. Festus' Fresh Coffee[75]: Festus has just brewed a fresh pot of coffee in the Marshal's Office and offers a cup to Doc: "Ughh...YUK! Oh, good heavens, that is the worst stuff I've ever tasted. That is poison! It's lethal! Matt, if you ever drink that, there's not an antidote known to medical science that'll take care of you! Know what I think Matt? I think he's got something against us! I think he's trying to get rid of us! I think he's trying to get your job! That's it," Doc yells.

"Pills with ah mouth, that's what ya are Doc! There ain't nobody say'n ya got'a drink it, is there Mathew?" "Matt, don't do it now, don't do it. I'll buy you a good cup of coffee at Delmonico's....come on!"(Doc). "Jist hold yer taters

---

[75] Various episodes with Festus Haggen from Season 12: 1966-67 through Season 20, 1974-75.

now, let Mathew make up his own mind by his ownself. He ain't even put ah taster on it yet! Go on, drink er down Mathew!"(Festus). "I warned you Matt!"(Doc). "Ughh… yuk, hack, hack…does that offer still hold Doc," Matt asks. "Now jist hold on! What am I supposed ta do with all this here fresh coffee Doc?"(Festus). "I don't think I could tell him Matt, lets go!"(Doc)

Prov. 14.10: The heart knows its own bitterness, and no stranger shares its joy.

Lk. 1.15: For he will be great before the Lord, and he shall drink no wine, nor strong drink, and he will be filled with the Holy Spirit, even from his mother's womb.

Prov. 31.6: Give strong drink to him who is perishing, and wine to those in bitter distress; let them drink and forget their poverty, and remember their misery no more.

26. Mule Headedness[76]: "Ah mule that won't move ain't no excusedness! Young'n yer git'n on that mule an yer go'n to turn around an head fer home," Festus tells the young girl who is running away from home. "He won't move any. I've been trying, but he just won't move," says the young girl. "Now before ya learn ah mule anything ya got'a know

---

76 1974-75: Season 20, Series No. 629, No. 18 in season, written by Herman Groves.

more an ah mule knows, now git on yer saddle! Now lookie here mule, do ya see this here big stick?"(Festus). "HEEE HAW!!" (The mule brays.) **"WAIT A MINUTE MULE! Yer supposed ta turn around an go the tother way!"(Festus)**

Ps. 38.13: But I am like a deaf man, I do not hear like a dumb man who does not open his mouth.

Prov. 1.1,4: The proverbs of Solomon, son of David, king of Israel: That men may know wisdom and instruction, understand words of insight, that prudence may be given to the simple, knowledge and discretion to the youth.

<u>27. Festus' Posse</u>[77]: Matt got seriously shot in his right arm by a gang of outlaws robbing the bank in Dodge, and after the incident, he decides to turn in his badge and leave town until he heals and practices shooting with his left arm. Festus excitedly scurries around to get up a posse to go after the outlaws, but Kitty and Doc think he should cool down and think through the situation:

"He's gone an I don't know when he'll be back if ever! Newly, ya go git Lathrop and Harvey an whoever else ya can find, an I'll git Jonas, Holmes, and Burk. Ya git anybody that can set ah saddle an tell em to bring ah horse, cuz I'm git'n ah posse tagether an go after em. Hi Miss

---

[77] 1973-74: Season 19, Series No. 590, No. 3 in season, written by Ron Bishop.

Kitty!"(Festus). "I don't think that is a good idea Festus," says Kitty. "What's not a good idea," asks Doc. "Doc, we ain't got time ta tell ya about it now. Whilst we're ah stand'n here an jaw'n, them yahoos are run'n after Mathew ta kill him! What do ya propose ta do about it?"(Festus). "STOP and think about it before you go off running like a chicken with its head cut off!"(Doc). "Well I'm tell'n ya I'm fix'n ta git up a posse an go after em!"

"Let's just calm down," says Kitty. "I agree with Festus, and we're going after them and going right now," says Newly. "Newly, you don't do anything until we think about it!"(Doc). "Doc, ya don't even know exactly what yer talk'n about!"(Festus). "I know exactly what you are talking about! You're talking about getting a posse together and go traipsing around the country with blood in your eye! Now lets talk about it first, but not out here in the street!"(Doc). "Doc, now ya jist don't understand!"(Festus). "Oh, I understand all right, and so does Kitty! Let me explain something. The reason Matt left in the first place is so an awful lot of people in Dodge wouldn't get hurt trying to protect him!"(Doc). "But this here ain't the same thing Doc. Don't ya see? I ain't never felt so hogtied in all my born days!"(Festus)

Prov. 23.29: Who has woe? Who has sorrow? Who has strife? Who has complaining? Who has wounds without cause? Who has redness of eyes?

Ecc. 8.9: All this I observed while applying my mind to all that is done under the sun, while man lords it over man to his hurt.

Jer. 6.24: We have heard the report of it, our hands fall helpless; anguish has taken hold of us, pain as of a woman in travail.

---

28. Temporary Marshal[78]: A new temporary Marshal comes to town to replace Matt while he heals from a gunshot wound. He comes into the office and sees Festus bent over an ironing board and a pile of clothes stacked on the desk:

"Get that stuff out of here," says the new Marshal. "Now ya don't have ta look so sourty in the face!"(Festus). "Is this the Marshal's office or a Chinese laundry? You get my telegram?"(Marshal). "We got it!"(Festus). "I said I was arriving on the morning stage! You didn't see fit to meet me!"(Marshal). "Ya know, I was jist plum shore that ya could find yer way ta the jail all by yer own self!"(Festus). "I favor a clean desk, here read this stack of papers and give me back what's important!"(Marshal). "Pffft, read these here papers! My eyes an ears is ah ache'n over ya already, I'll git Newly ta help me out on this quagmireness of papers directly!"(Festus)

---

78 1971-72: Season 17, Series No. 547, No. 8 in season, written by Ron Bishop.

Is. 28.11: Nay, but by men of strange lips and with an alien tongue the Lord will speak to this people.

Deut. 31.11: When all Israel comes to appear before the Lord God at the place that he will choose, you shall read this law before all Israel in their hearing.

Rev. 1.3: Blessed is he who reads aloud the words of the prophecy, and blessed are those who hear, and who keep what is written therein; for the time is near.

---

29. Doc's Rescue[79]: Matt, Festus, and Newly are venturing into the wild country of New Mexico to rescue Doc and his woman friend from outlaws that kidnapped him to give medical attention to their leader's (Shindle) son who was stabbed by another member of the gang in a fight over a woman's attention. They arrive in a small adobe town with a wagonload of cavalry rifles, pretending to be gun run traders. A few hours prior, they were confronted by members of the outlaw gang that intended to bushwhack them on the trail, and half the bushwhackers were shot down. Shindle asks how it is that his men got ambushed and killed and Festus starts talking:

---

79 1974-75: Season 20, Series No. 614-615, No. 3-4 in season, written by Paul Savage.

"No they wasn't no ambush, yer boys ain't noth'n but ah bunch of mangy bushwhackers their own selves, it was nose ta nose mister and yer boys was ah look'n fer trouble an the onlyest thing was they was jist ah tad bit slow!" "You mean to tell me you shot down half of my men and never got a scratch on you three?" Montero was the best gun fighter I had," says Shindle. "Yup he was about the best I ever see'd too, 'cept'n ya know it pretty much makes ah feller wonder which best feller he was, with him be'n one of the best an all, an they was no way of tell'n which one of us was that took him rightly blame on his broadsides!"(Festus)

"What's your name," Shindle asks. "What ever's friendly," says Festus. "Perhaps you three maybe should join up with us!"(Shindle). "What makes ya think we orta trust ya?"(Festus). "Well for one thing you're taking a big risk riding in here surrounded by my men, and back out there along those boulders and hills there's Apache raiders just dying to lay their hands on you!"(Shindle). "To tell ya the truth, my ole scalp's been ah itch'n ever since we been traips'n in Capache country!"(Festus). "We'll think on it," says Matt.

Festus wanders over to the town well when he sees Doc over there getting a drink and Doc's looking his way and Festus speaks up: **"Now right there's ah looksome sight! I'm so blamed parched I can't even pucker. I'm ah think'n I'll wet my whistle!"** Festus whispers to Doc: **"Now Doc, Mathew's got that there git'n outa here all worked out.**

When it's dark the Commancheros will be ah jump'n every which way all liquored up an such. We can do it Doc an we's about ta pull outa this hornets nest in the wee hour of morn'n. The onlyest thing ya got ta do Doc, is stay in yer buggy with yer woman friend when it's time an we'll take care of the rest." "Now listen Festus there's something I want to say to you. If this thing don't come out the way we want it to, I want to say...."(Doc). "Hold on ya old scudder, ya ain't gunna start git'n all syrupy on me are ya?"(Festus). "You didn't let me finish! What I want to say is, if it don't come out right....well, well, I...well, it'll probably be because you bungled it!"(Doc). "Pffttt! Well that there is more like it! Pfftt!"(Festus)

Matt decides the best thing to do is to pretend to join up with Shindle, and that will give him time to develop a plan for rescuing Doc and get out of there. At the evening dinner he tells Shindle they'll join up, and Festus starts his usual yammering: **"I'll tell ya this Mister Shindle it jist shames the hair off'n ah hog with that boy oh your'n rode clean through the war of the 'CAUSE' an then git'n back jaw stabbed by his own friend!"**

Doc's lady friend comes in the room to serve up the meal: **Festus says, "Well don't she look lairip'n? Well don't jist stand there missy, bring er on down here an let's git started ah eat'n. Ah feller could starve ta death jist sit'n here ah wait'n fer ya! Here, ya better let me take that platter, it looks kinda heavy! Wooop! Ya spilled it ya danged knot-head. I'll tell ya, it's been many ah day since I put in ta vitals like this here fer my ole gullet …heh..heh! Hey feller would ya swamp my way some oh that sopp'n gravy there? I'll tell ya, I may need me ah bushel er two of biscuits before I git done sopp'n all this here gravy!" "You keep feed'n us like this we may just have to change our minds about joining up with you Shindle," says Matt. "Ya bet'cha Mr. Shindle, ya jist name it; banks, stages, cattle….heh..heh, it sure beats the way we been scroung'n for ah liv'n up ta now don't it?"(Festus). Latter that night, Matt, Festus, and Newly rescue Doc and his lady friend, kill the bandits, blow up their compound, and clear out for Kansas.

Prov. 11.3: The integrity of the upright guides them, but the crookedness of the treacherous destroys them.

Prov. 24.11: Rescue those who are being taken away to death; hold back those who are stumbling to the slaughter.

Jn. 15.13: "Greater love has no man than this, that a man lay down his life for his friends."

---

30. Drover Wil[80]: "That ole drover Wil an his breed is git'n scarce Mathew. When them trail herds quit come'n through Dodge things is go'n ta git jist plumed out ain't they?"

---

80 1974-75: Season 20, Series No. 616, No. 5 in season, written by Jim Byrnes.

"Things are changing Festus and those drovers that won't change along with it will be left out in the cold," says Matt.

"Sweat'n dirt cowboys all their born days have one run-in with ah knot head an here all of ah sudden they's outlaws. Mathew, could we let em jist keep ride'n off ta Texas instead of chase'n after em? Fact is, the onlyest thing they's wanted fer was fer taken twelve dollars an ah shoot'n, then the other feller went an shot at em first! Tarnation, they's likely go'n ta pay it back rightly anyways when they gits things even'd out. Don't ya see? He orta jist keep ride'n. Ole Wil ain't changed none ah bit, ah be'n on the run has he?"(Festus)

"Still ah ram-rod'n, take'n care of his men," Matt says. "Him an ole Quincy were jist about as close't as two men gits."(Festus). "Yes, jist like Wil isn't it? Wouldn't let Quincy die of that gunshot wound til he got him back to Texas," says Matt. "Ole Wil will be figger'n this'll be his bury'n ground too won't he Mathew?" "I know Festus." "Afraid it's jist like we called it Mathew, he ain't run'n an he ain't come'n back!"

Just then Will bolted his horse toward a herd of cattle and stampeded them right into himself and was trampled to death: "Noth'n ya could 'a did about it. That there was a fool thing there that Wil done ah ride'n headlong into that stampede'n herd, but he wouldn't had it no other way. Ya know, it's jist like he said about hoof'n it ta Texas. He's ah go'n home!"(Festus)

Prov. 16.26: A worker's appetite works for him; his mouth urges him on.

Is. 1.5: Why will you still be smitten, that you continue to rebel? The whole head is sick, and the whole heart faint.

Jer. 21.8: "And to this people you shall say": 'Thus, says the Lord, "Behold, I set before you the way of life and the way of death."

---

31. <u>Family of Outlaws</u>[81]: The Kaysinger family promised to get even with Judge Kendall who sentenced their son and brother Carey to hang by his neck until dead the following morning, but the Judge, who is dying of heart failure has his own plan:

"Good morn'n judge!" "Good morning Festus!" "Yer up kinda early ain't ya?" "No, I didn't sleep very well so I thought I'd might as well come over and go through some of my papers." "Can I git ya ah cup of coffee?" "No thanks Festus, but may I use your desk?" "Well of course! Go ahead on, I ain't been do'n noth'n but rest'n my feet on it all night!" "Where's Matt and Newly?"(Judge). "Well they

---
81 1974-75: Season 20, Series No. 621, No. 10 in season, written by Wm. Keys.

went on over to Delmonico's ta eat breakfast."(Festus). "Why don't you go over and join them?"(Judge). "No, I reckon I better stay here and keep my eyeball peeled on Carey Kaysinger!" "Oh, I can do that, I'll be here anyway, just go ahead."(Judge). "Well much obliged ta ya judge. I reckon I could stand ah little biscuits an red-eye gravy, ah little grits, eggs and ham..heh..heh. See ya right shortly judge!"(Festus).

Ecc. 3.16: Moreover I saw under the sun that in the place of justice even there was wickedness, and in the place of righteousness, even there was wickedness.

―⸺

The Judge, according to his plan, let Carey Kaysinger out of jail while pretending to take him to Hayes to be hanged while Festus and Matt were having breakfast over at Delmonicos. The Judge took Carey by horse and buggy to lure his dad and brothers and used himself as bait. In a gunfight the Judge managed to kill Carey outside of Dodge, and his brothers and dad killed the Judge. Matt and Festus saw them leave Dodge and in hot pursuit came upon the gunfight and killed the Kaysinger brothers and wounded old man Kaysinger who lays on the ground with Festus over the top of him: **"Where's my boys," gasped old man Kaysinger. "They's dead Kaysinger, but you'll live long enough ta hang yer own self," says Festus. "The Judge, he done it all Mathew. He set em up so as ta kill** him, an then he got them in the end!"(Festus). "I reckon that's just what he did Festus."(Matt). "Men like them there Kaysingers never will understand the law an men like Judge Kendall, and that's a pure o'lee fact."(Festus)

Prov. 1.3: Receive instruction in wise dealing, righteousness, justice, and equity.

Is. 66.16: For by fire will the Lord execute judgment, and by his sword, upon all flesh; and those slain by the Lord shall be many.

32. Festus' Prisoner[82]: Matt and Festus are taking a prisoner (Dixon) to jail at Cottonwood Springs. Matt returns to Dodge while Festus stays on in Cottonwood:

"Looks like ole Ruth is limping a little bit Festus," says Matt. "Appears like it Mathew. Looks like ah tendern swolled up. I'll have ta hole up here and rest him ah day er two. Come on ya jailbird, git in here ta the jail house an quit yer drag'n yer feet!" "So long Festus!"(Mathew). "Take care of yerself Mathew," says Festus.

"Folks are all ready for Dixon's hang'n tomorrow, and folks are working on the gallows today," says the Cottonwood Sheriff. "I sure am tickled ta git shed ah him. I come

---

[82] 1974-75: Season 20, Series No. 622-623, No. 11-12 in season, written by Jim Byrnes.

within ah whisker of shoot'n him twice already!"(Festus). "Well I'm glad you didn't. This hang'n is going to cost the taxpayers, but it'll be as welcome as rain. He killed the Cactus Springs bank clerk, and folks here liked him. Seems your going to be in town a spell Festus, and I'd like to buy you a beer," says the Sheriff. "Well now, I could use me ah cold beer, I'll tell ya that Sheriff."(Festus). "After you stable that mule, I'll meet you at the Union Belle, it's the best food in town," says the Sheriff. "Us Haggens got an eye fer good vitals. I'll be there rightly. Come on Ruth! Come on ole feller ya can make it on yer own self!"(Festus)

Ps. 107.10: Some sat in darkness and in glom, prisoners in affliction and in irons, for they had rebelled against the words of God, and spurned the counsel of the Most High.

33. Ruth Gets Sold[83]: A young man came to Dodge City to buy a mule to plow his field with and he was conned by a man who sold him Festus' mule, Ruth. Festus drew his gun and caught the young man as he was starting to ride out of town, but in a struggle to get him off of his mule, Festus accidentally shot the young man in the foot. The shot brought Matt and Doc on the scene:

---

83 1974-75: Season 20, Series No. 635, No. 24 in season, written by Earl W. Wallace.

"Hey ya git yer carcass off'n that mule, ya hear me," says Festus. "What fer," says Able, the young man. " 'Cause it's Ruth my mule!"(Festus). "This is my mule. I just bought it off of a fella!"(Able). "I ain't go'n ta tell ya no more, ya git yerself off'n my mule!"(Festus)

BANG! Festus' gun goes off and hits the young man in the leg: "Too bad Festus wasn't trying to hit you, you'd been standing there in the street without a scratch," Doc says to Able. "Aw! Ya blamed ole scudder mind yer ownself's business!"(Festus). "Young man, you got a bill of sale for that mule," Matt asks. "Yes here it is!"(Able). "You can't read can you? What you have here is an old handbill for a steam bath in New Orleans," says Matt. "I was wonder'n why there'd be a picture of a pretty lady on it."(Able). "Don't fret none about git'n home young feller, I'll see that ya git there all right," Festus tells Able.

Prov. 13.16: In everything a prudent man acts with knowledge, but a fool flaunts his folly.

―⤴―

Out of guilt and compassion for the young man, Festus took him back home where he came from: **"Whoa Ruth!"**(Festus). "Who ya got there son," asks Abel's father. "He ain't got nobody! I jist brung'd him home. You his pa are ya?"(Festus). "Well that kinda depends. He ain't done noth'n unlawful has he?" "NO! He ain't done noth'n wrong! Ya see there was this little accident where he kind'a got ah bullet in his leg there, and me is the one that shot him."(Festus)

"I can tell ya what happened there, ya see yer young'n ran into ah slipperty yahoo there in town an he jist got shucked clean out'a his money by spend'n yer money buy'n ole Ruth here, and I feel like I owe the young feller someth'n see'ns I was the one that shot him in the leg. Where do ya want me ta put yer boy? I got'a be git'n back ta Dodge!"(Festus). "Well now don't be in a hurry to be leave'n," says the father. "Whoa there now ya jist back-up! If yer think'n what I'm think'n yer think'n, I ain't go'n ta be hitch'n my mule to yer plow! That dog won't hunt!"(Festus)

Prov. 6.6-7: Go to the ant, O sluggard; consider her ways, and be wise. Without having any chief officer or ruler, she prepares her food in summer, and gathers her sustenance in harvest.

Prov. 13.4: The soul of the sluggard craves, and gets nothing, while the soul of the diligent is richly supplied.

34. The Good Samaritan[84]:
"Howdy young'n! How'd ya git here," asks Festus. "My horse was spooked by a rattler an ran off," says the boy. "This here ain't no place ta be

---

84 1974-75: Season 20, Series No. 626, No. 15 in season, written by Paul Savage.

afoot!"(Festus). "I'll get by," says the boy. "Ha! I always figgered a feller that felt that way about it will git by. I ain't never see'd ya before don't believe!"(Festus). "Just pass'n through and taken hides an such," says the boy. "That so! Well it's ah sorry thing this ole drought, awful hurt'n ah lot ah good folks. Sit down if ya want ta. Got ah lot ah prairie chicken here on the spit, an more'n I can eat by my ownself."(Festus)

"There's no need," says the boy. "There ain't no need not to neither! Suit yerself! I'll tell ya I jist like ta tarry out'a town now an then. I jist can't stand be'n around town too long, but there's one thing about ah town. There's always room fer one more!"(Festus). The boy sits down and eats with Festus: "Well thanks for the eats, I guess I'll be go'n on!"(Boy). "I'm fix'n ta be head'n that way directly. Ole Ruth himself'll ride double I reckon. Leastwise we can test him!"(Festus). "Well my shoes does have holes in em," says the boy. "That there offer still goes!"(Festus). "Thanks mister. What's yer name again," the boy asks. "Festus Haggen!"

Is. 65.2: I spread out my hands all the day to a rebellious people, who walk in a way that is not good, following their own devices.

Jer. 6.16: Thus says the Lord: "Stand by the roads, and look, and ask for the ancient paths, where the good way is; and walk in it, and find rest for your souls." But they said, "We will not walk in it."

35. Doc's Prized Fishing Pole[85]: Doc is talking to Festus about many people in Dodge ready to help people in need after Festus spent the good part of two weeks doing that very thing, and just then the young man he was helping out comes along and asks him if they are going fishing Saturday:

"Good heavens Festus there's enough folks around here to help a fellow out without you taking it all upon yourself," says Doc.

"Hey Festus are we go'n fish'n Saturday," asks the young boy Festus befriended and brought to town. "Oh course we are!"(Festus). "FISH'N! Now what's this about fish'n?"(Doc). "Well I was jist fix'n ta ask ya if I could borry yer fish'n pole."(Festus). "You mean to tell me you have the unmitigated gall to stand there and ask me to borrow my fishing pole?"(Doc). "Well shoot Doc I ain't gonna hurt it none!" "Course not, cause your not even going to touch it! Not with gloves on! Now on the other hand if you would like to borrow it for the young fella, I would be delighted! Just as long as he doesn't let you LOOK AT IT!"(Doc). "Nee, nee, nee jist as long as ya don't let me look at it! Ya stingy ole scudder! I don't give ah hoot! I'll cut me ah 'willer' pole and dig me ah hand full ah worms and I'll catch more fish an ya did in yer whole blamed life! Pffttt!"

---

85 1974-75: Season 20, Series No. 626, No. 15 in season, written by Paul Savage.

Prov. 22.7: The rich rules over the poor, and the borrower is the slave of the lender.

Ps. 37.21: The wicked borrows, and cannot pay back, but the righteous is generous and gives:

---

36. Festus Will Show Up[86]: Doc & Matt are in the Long Branch talking about the coming square dance gala on the weekend and Burk the organizer comes in and asks if Festus is going to be back in time to call the square dance:

"Every time I see a free drink being handed out I think of Festus," says Doc. "Now Matt, is Festus going to be here to call the square dance on Saturday night or not," asks Burk. "He said he'd be here and I wouldn't doubt him one minute!"(Matt). "I've got a million things to take care of and I can't be worrying about who the caller is going to be!"(Burk). "Now Festus may stop and do a little fish'n along the way, but if you think he is going to miss a chance to strut around in front of the whole town you're mistaken! Burk you've got a million things to think about and two is too many," says Doc.

Prov. 11.2: When pride comes, then comes disgrace; but with the humble is wisdom.

---

86 1971-72: Season 17, Series No. 557, No. 18 in season, written by Wm. Kelley.

Prov. 15.22: Without counsel plans go wrong, but with many advisers they succeed.

Prov. 21.5: The plans of the diligent lead surely to abundance, but everyone who is hasty comes only to want.

Jer. 13.15: Hear and give ear; be not proud, for the Lord has spoken.

---

37. Festus & the Preacher[87]: Festus encounters a retired elderly preacher who's dream is to build a church and minister the Christian faith to the Comanche on their Reservation and Nestatoga town folks don't like the idea and don't want the church built:

"Ya know if ah feller ever was ta git ah church built ah start'n off the way yer do'n it, chances are the first stout wind would come along an blow it down right around the preacher's ears, an it might even wake up the whole congregation!" "It doesn't look like much does it."(Preacher). "No sir, it don't. Don't ya think Reverend it's about time fer ya admit'n ya can't do it by yer ownself?" "I'll do it," says the Preacher. "Fiddle, I know'd what's ya gonna say before I even asked ah question. Ya know I was think'n right back here it wouldn't do no good if ah whole herd ah

---

[87] 1974-75: Season 20, Series No. 632, No. 21 in season, written by Wm. Putman.

angels come right down from the Pearlity Gates an give ya that same advice that I gave ya! That's the kind ah stubbern ole…..beg yer pardon Reverend. I guess I got disrespectfulness there fer ah minute," says Festus.

Festus starts gathering boards to build the framing: **"What do you think you are doing?"**(Preacher) **"I'm fix'n ta help ya build this here church an I ain't ask'n fer no pay ah do'n it!"**(Festus). **"Well I guess I am up a creek without a paddle on this church building."**(Preacher). **"Well I'm up the crick with ya this far with ya Reverend, I might as well paddle the rest ah the way! My mind's done made up!"**

Prov. 9.1: Wisdom has built her house, she has set up her seven pillars.

Prov. 14.1: Wisdom builds her house, but folly with her own hands tears it down.

Several days pass and the two of them have the walls framed-in and a roof on the church: **"Well looks like we got er jist about all built Reverend!"**(Festus). **"You've been very generous with your time Festus Haggen. Deputy, I'd like to give you something."**(Preacher). **"No! I done told ya once't I ain't do'n noth'n fer no pay and I mean it!"** **"This is a remembrance I'd like you to have."** **"Why I couldn't take yer**

watch Reverend. Onlyest watch I ever saw couldn't hold ah candle ta that there'n yer offer'n me was in ah mail order book an it cost pret'n nye thirty dollars!" "Well I'm sure this one cost much more than thirty dollars. It was given to me by my Bishop on the occasion of my retirement." Ya orta be ashamed of yerself ah try'n ta give me away ah gift that was gave ta ya!"(Festus). "I'd like you to have it just the same, so take it and no more talking on it!"(Preacher)

Ps. 127.1: Unless the Lord builds the house, those who build it labor in vain. Unless the Lord watches over the city, the watchman stays awake in vain.

1Cor. 14.12: So with yourselves; since you are eager for manifestations of the Spirit, strive to excel in building up the church.

Soon after the church is built, a group of men from Nestatogo came on Saturday night and burned down the church while Festus and the Preacher were sleeping. Festus rode into the town and walked into the town church on Sunday morning while the town preacher was delivering his sermon. Festus walked down the aisle and said what was on his mind:

"Well, I'll be ah tall oak! Now hold on preacher, jist be'n ah preacher an ah herd'n folks tor'd the truth an light, that there would account for someth'n, but there's some

ornry no good knot heads around here that need more an ah talk'n to!" "What do you want sir, barging in here while I'm giving my sermon to my town flock?"(Preacher Atkins)

"Jist fer the time be'n I'll jist figger ya don't know what happened last night!" "What are you talking about? What happened last night?"(Atkins). "I'll guarantee ya there's some of yer flock knows what happened last night!"(Festus). "Whatever is bothering you, this is never the time nor place!"(Preacher Atkins). "What ya mean is, this is the mainest place preacher! Ya don't go ah tromp'n on ah man's dreams an not git called fer it! Now I ain't no preacher, an I ain't had me no school learn'n a'tall what so ever. What I'm fix'n ta say here might not be the fit'n proper words, but I figger you'll all git what I mean!"

"I want ta tell ya about ah man, worked hard all his life ah preach'n the Gospel, mostly ta ah bunch ah people who done no practice'n on it cept'n fer ah hour or two on Sundays, like I got ah figger'n ah lot ah you folks does. Now this here man tried ta do good all his life, an one day he got old an them that runs his church figger'd he wasn't no good ah hoot ta nobody, so they run him off. Now he didn't figger he was done, not by ah long shot, so he went ta look'n around every place ah try'n an figger'n out somebody that he could help. Finally he done come clean out here from the east ah want'n ta build ah church fer the Injuns!"

"Whether he was crazy or whether he wasn't, that's what he wanted ta do. He done it all by his ownself with the help oh the Lord. He spent ever last penny he had ah do'n it an I figger he had a right ta give it ah whirl. To try it, he come right here ta yer town in Nestatoga, wanted to do good an he got his self good'n tromped on by some of ya righteous God fear'n folks!"

"Now all of ya didn't strike the match that set his church on fire last night, but ya was ah egg'n on the ones that done it, and the mainest one is yer preacher Atkins here! Preacher Atkins, I figger there's ah right an there's ah wrong. Appears ah lot oh yer flock here don't know which is which, an have'n em decide which is which is yer job! Or ain't nobody ever told ya that! That's all I got ta say!" Festus turned and walked down the aisle and out the door. The next day Atkins and his flock came and rebuilt the church.

Prov. 16.18: Pride goes before a fall, and a haughty spirit before a fall.

Prov. 14.11: The house of the wicked will be destroyed, but the tent of the upright will flourish.

38. Silas Killed Ah Dead Man[88]: "Hey fellas is the Marshal around," asks Silas Shute. "Ya he's around. Why?"(Festus). "My name's Silas Shute. I'm here ta collect my reward on this feller draped over my burro!" "You ah bounty hunter are ya? Who ya got there?"(Festus). "His name is Jake Daniels!"(Silas). "Where'd ya git him?"(Festus). "In Morenco country!"(Silas). "Out by the Rucker spread?"(Festus). "I wish I could'a bring'd him in breath'n, but he put up a fight, tried ta make ah break for it and I killed him with one shot!" "I'm pretty handy with this here thing!"(Silas)

"Festus, look it here, isn't this Jed Bailey," asks Doc. "Well look at that, course it is. Well it sure enough is," says Festus. "Course it is, WHAT?"(Silas). "This here's Jed Bailey! He ain't Jake Daniels!"(Festus). "Mister ya just take a look here on this Wanted Poster and tell me that this feller is Jed Bailey and not Jake Daniels!"(Silas) "He does look ah good bit like Jed Bailey don't he Mathew?"(Festus). "Yes there is a resemblance there all right."(Matt). "Mister I hate to tell you this, but the man you killed is not Jake Daniels! The man you killed is Jed Bailey and he's not a wanted man!"(Matt). "He ain't Daniels? Why the poster looks just like him!"(Silas). "Appears yer hunt'n days is over mister! Ya jist killed yerself ah innocent man is what ya done! Let's go!"(Festus)

---

[88] 1966-67: Season 12, Series No. 414, No. 5 in season, written by James Landis.

"Marshal it's about time I started tell'n ya the truth I guess! I really didn't kill him!"(Silas). "What?"(Festus). "I said I didn't kill him!"(Silas) "Whoa now, jist hold on there! Now out yonder ya told me an ole Doc and Nathan Burk that ya did kill him!"(Festus). "I don't care what you and Doc and whoever it was hear'd what I said. I didn't kill him! He was already dead when I found him ah hang'n from ah tree!"(Silas). "Hang'n from ah tree?"(Festus). "Right, I just was ride'n along when I see this feller hang'n from ah tree so I rode up where I could git a better look at him and he looked just like Jake Daniels!"(Silas). "Wait jist ah minute! Are ya try'n to tell us that ya found ah man ah hang'n from ah tree already dead an ya cut him down an shot him?"(Festus). "That's just what I done!"(Silas) "Pfftt!"(Festus)

Prov. 30.8: Remove far from me falsehood and lying; give me neither poverty nor riches; feed me with the food that is needful for me.

Prov. 13.21: Misfortune pursues sinners, but prosperity rewards the righteous.

Ps. 119.29: Put false ways far from me; and graciously teach me thy law!

39. Festus' Prisoner, Silas: Festus is tending to the prisoner, Silas Shute, at the Dodge City jail: "When does a feller git someth'n ta eat around here," Silas asks. "Ya git someth'n ta eat when the vitals gits here, that's when!"(Festus). "While we is wait'n fer em why don't ya git me a little bit of elixir?"(Silas). "I told ya time and time agin that Mathew don't allow no lixer in the jail house! Now I mean it!"(Festus). "This ain't fer drink'n Festus, it's fer my wheez'n!"(Silas). "Wheez'n! Ha! Ya orn'ry ole scamp you!"(Festus). "Who you call'n old?"(Silas). "You that's who!"(Festus). "I can see right now I ain't fix'n ta git a fair trial in this town!"(Silas). "You is jist blame lucky ta git ah trial a'tall I'll tell ya that!"(Festus). "That feller got himself hung by somebody else I told ya!"(Silas). "Oh ya, course he did an by his own rope too!"(Festus)

"Somebody took that rope and whoever took it knows I'm ah innocent man! I'm just left ta rot here in this rotten jail oh yers!"(Silas). "That rigs it! Now how could ya be ah rotten in jail, ya ain't been here but ah couple hours an don't ya go call'n this here jail rotten er I'll git on ya like ugly on ah ape!"(Festus). "You just try it and I'll knock knots on yer head fast'rn you can rub em!"(Silas). "Pffttt!"(Festus)

Prov. 27.7: He who is sated loathes honey, but to one who is hungry everything bitter is sweet.

Prov. 31.6-7: Give strong drink to him who is perishing, and wine to those in bitter distress; Let them drink and forget their poverty, and remember their misery no more.

"Marshal Dillon can I ask ya someth'n?"(Silas Shute). "What's that Silas?"(Matt). "Make that Festus feller give a little elixir will ya?"(Silas). "Oh I guess you can give him a little Festus. I'll be back later."(Matt). "Well whatever ya say Mathew, but I don't know why yer given this ole scudder his way about it. There ain't nobody else ever had whiskey in the jailhouse before and I specially don't know why ya would let this here skagy one have it! I want ya ta know this is the very firstest time that Mathew has ever let anybody have lixer in here!"(Festus). "Would you have a little swaller Festus?"(Silas) "NO! The smell of it, and of you is a'plenty fer me!"(Festus)

"How's ole Whitey?"(Silas). "What'd ya mean by that?"(Festus). "My burro gits the sags when he gits lonesome. He worries ah lot."(Silas). "Well that's ah funny thing, ole Ruth does that too!"(Festus). "Ruth?"(Silas). "Ruth, my mule! Ya don't have ta fret about yer's cause Ruth out yonder is ah keep'n yer's company!"(Festus). "He is?"(Silas). "He is! They is down there in the livery jist ah mush'n it up someth'n fierce! They's ah nuzzle'n and rub'n one another like they's ole friends."(Festus)

Ps. 60.3: Thou has made thy people suffer hard things; thou has given us wine to drink that made us reel.

Prov. 15.33: The fear of the Lord is instruction in wisdom, and humility goes before honor.

―❦―

40. Silas Is Not Guilty: The men who killed Jed Bailey came into Dodge and confessed to Matt and Silas is a free man: **"Festus, get Silas out of here will ya? He has been cleared of those hanging charges,"** says Matt. **"All right mister foot-in-the-mouth git ah git'n! Go on, an keep yer chin ta the wind!"(Festus)**

Prov. 15.30: The light of the eyes rejoices the heart, and good news refreshes the bones.

―❦―

41. Mathew & Kitty are Gone[89]**:** Kitty was kidnapped by a vengeful widow who's husband was convicted and hung for murder, and Matt was the one who caught him and arrested him. The widow and her sons are bent on exacting the same fate on Matt by using Kitty and Doc as bait to draw him to their ranch. When Matt found out the situation, he went after Kitty on his own:

---

[89] 1966-67: Season 12, Series No. 412, No. 3 in season, written by Hal Sitowitz.andis.

"Festus! Take off those spurs or sit down, your pacing back and forth on the floor is making me nervous," says Doc. "Golly Bill Doc I'm worried!"(Festus). "Well so am I!"(Doc). "First Kitty come up miss'n an now Mathew. They went someplace, but who knows where!"(Festus). "He's probably out looking for that outlaw!"(Doc). "Naw he wouldn't do that, cause if he was ta do that, I was ta be with him. He told me that!" (Festus). "Well where ever he went, he went in ah hurry! He has done it before, but not like this!"(Doc). "Well fiddle, we can't stand around here ah guess'n all day!"(Festus)

"The fact is Miss Kitty is gone and now Mathew's gone and I'm fix'n ta do someth'n about it!"(Festus). "Like what?"(Doc). "We're go'n ta git ah search'n party tagether an go out yonder look'n! Burk git down there ta the Long Branch an git Sam an the boys an whoever else ya can find and I'll meet ya back here in five minutes! Doc, I'm go'n over ta Delmonico's and do the same thing!"(Festus). "Whoa now, Festus why don't you wait til tomorrow morning?"(Doc). "WAIT?"(Festus). "It's going to be dark in a couple of hours!"(Doc) "Well so it gits dark!"(Festus)

Prov. 20.22: Do not say, "I will repay evil"; wait for the Lord, and he will help you.

Is. 63.5: I looked, but there was no one to help; I was appalled, but there was no one to uphold; so my own arm brought me victory, and my wrath upheld me.

---

42. Matt's Resignation[90]: Matt tracked an outlaw for two weeks and finally caught up to him. He rode into Dodge with the dead outlaw draped over the man's horse. Matt is upset with himself for accidentally shooting the outlaw, an old friend and fellow Union soldier from the Civil War who was down and out and on the run from the law for stealing a horse and robbing some homesteaders. Matt was so upset with himself that he resigned as U.S. Marshal:

"Hold on a minute Festus! I want you to hear it from me. You are going to have a new Marshal in town! I'm resigning," says Matt. "What? Resignering? What in the Sam-Hell er ya talk'n about? Ya can't jist up an quit!"(Festus). "I just soon drop it Festus!" "Mathew, you jist slow down! Yer ah go'n too fast!" "Festus, I'm tired and want to get some sleep!"(Matt). "Well golly be, ya can't say such ah thing as that, then go ta sleep on it! This here takes jaw'n about an ah think'n on!"(Festus). "I've been thinking about it bringing a dead man fifty miles across the prairie on a stolen horse!"(Matt). "Well fiddle ya did that ah **100 times before**, what's different about this here one? What happened out

---

90 1966-67: Season 12, Series No. 410, No. 1 in season, written by Richard Carr.

there Mathew?"(Festus). "I want to get some sleep now will you get out of here and leave me alone?"(Matt). "Yer turn'n in yer badge don't make ah bit ah sense! Mathew, if ya need anything, you jist holler cause I'll be close't around."(Festus)

After a period of time with the new Marshal, who fired Festus so he could pick his own deputy, Matt had second thoughts. Especially when he had no authority to kick known bad men out of town that were drifting into Dodge when they heard he was no longer the Marshal. Matt withdrew his resignation and pinned his badge back on, and reinstated Festus as deputy.

Prov. 25.2: It is the glory of God to conceal things, but the glory of kings is to search things out.

Ecc. 11.10: Remove vexation from your mind, and put away pain from your body; for youth and the dawn of life are vanity.

43. Vacation for Matt & Festus[91]: "I jist got'a git some rest Doc, I been ah work'n too dang hard," Festus says to Doc. "I'd like to know what at?"(Doc). "Mathew! I can recommend that **YOU** get away for a few days, I'll tell you that!"(Doc). "I've been thinking about it Doc. Festus, what do you say you and I saddle up and head into the high country for a few days and do a little hunting!"(Matt). "Well

---

91 Various episodes with Festus Haggen from Season 12: 1966-67 through Season 20, 1974-75.

now, good idea, we'll jist saddle up an ride up in the high country an do us a little hunt'n! Mathew and me!"(Festus). "I'm in favor of it just as long as it doesn't get to be a habit," says Kitty. "Ah fiddle Dodge is the onlyest habit we got ain't it Mathew?"(Festus). "You bet Festus!"(Matt)

Ps. 23.1-3: The Lord is my shepherd, I shall not want; he makes me lie down in green pastures. He leads me beside still waters; He restores my soul. He leads me in paths of righteousness for His name's sake.

---

44. Where Ya Go'n Mathew?[92]: "Mathew now ya listen ta me. They ain't no reason on the good Lord's green earth that ya can't take ya a few days off. Ya know those drovers is left town an ole Harley Skinner's trial don't come up til next month, ana the town's as quiet as a parson's Sunday parlor," Festus says. "You've been putting in some long days Matt."(Doc). "There ain't ah thing come'n up that me an ole Thad couldn't take care of. We've did it ah hundred times before! Nobody'd have ta tell me ta take ah rest and relax, I'll tell ya that!"(Festus). "Is that a fact!"(Matt). "Ask your doctor I could tell you that you sure need…"(Doc). "Well even ah GOOD doctor would tell ya that ah man can't keep ah run'n around and ah work'n no more an ah grand daddy clock can ah keep ah tick'n all…"(Festus).

---

92 Ibid.

"HAVE YOU FINISHED?" (Doc). "Well I'm jist try'n…"(Festus). "I know what you're trying to do, you're trying to drive me crazy! NOW HUSH, JUST HUSH! Matt how long has it been since you took a day off?"(Doc). "Well matter of fact it's been awhile Doc."(Matt). "Well that's what I mean. As your doctor, and at the risk of agreeing with Festus, tell you what you do. Go fish'n!"(Doc). "Well that's jist"….(Festus). "Your horse is all saddled ready to go Matt!"(Doc)

"Well where ya go'n now Mathew?"(Festus). "Well I see a farewell committee is all here."(Kitty). "Farewell committee?"(Doc). "What ya talk'n about Miss Kitty, are ya go'n somewhere?"(Festus). "No, but Matt is!" (Kitty). "Oh, Mathew where ya go'n?"(Festus). "Oh I thought I might go up to the White Oak Creek."(Matt). "What?"(Festus). "Yep, do a little fish'n and say hello to Caleb!"(Matt). "Why in tarnation didn't you say so!"(Doc). "Yeh, ya let me run off at the mouth here all morn'n!"(Festus). "I tried to say something back around Aunt Tanzy's buried husband and was going to leave right after you finished!"(Matt). "Finished what?"(Kitty)

"Well Matt you better get outa here or he's going to get started again! Bring me a big catfish about two feet long, about like that will ya?"(Doc). "All right Doc. See you in a few days Kitty!"(Matt). "Have a good time!"(Kitty). "Don't give anything ah second thought, no sir Mathew don't ya fret about ah thing, cause there ain't ah come'n up that can't be taken care of twixt Thad an me, I'll guarantee ya that!"(Festus)

Prov. 8.14: I have counsel and sound wisdom, I have insight, I have strength.

Prov. 15.22: Without counsel plans go wrong, but with many advisers they succeed.

---

45. Festus' Gold Piece[93]: Doc and Festus are at the bar in the Long Branch: **"What are you looking for Festus?"(Doc). "I had me ah nickel here someplace." "I wish I had a nickel for every time you've looked for that!"(Doc). "Pfftt! Smart Alec look at that!"**

Festus slams a coin on the bar: **"A TEN DOLLAR GOLD PIECE! Where in thunder did you get that?"(Doc). "Well I got it fer paint'n Oley Goodson's barn, that's where!"(Festus). "Ten dollars for painting a little ole barn?"(Doc). "Little ole barn my foot, that's the biggest barn I ever saw. It took me near three days ta paint that an that's from sun-up ta sun-down. I'll tell ya this Doc, they ain't nobody that can paint ah barn like ah Haggen! Now ya take my uncle Hogan Haggen, he could paint ah**

---

[93] 1966-67: Season 12, Series No. 416, No. 7 in season, written by Robert Lewin.

barn before ya could say, 'ah rat ran across the roof with ah piece of raw liver in his mouth', and that's ah o'lee fact!"

Jer. 22.13: "Woe to him who builds his house by unrighteousness, and his upper rooms by injustice; who makes his neighbor serve him for nothing, and does not give him his wages."

⸻

46. Down & Out Whooly[94]: "Howdy Whooly," says Festus. "Howdy Festus, Doc, I been look'n around for Mr. Pervice, have ya seen him?" (Whooly). "No, wasn't in his store was he?"(Doc). "No he wasn't Doc. I got'a see him, but I don't think he wants ta see me." "How much you owe him Whooly?"(Doc). "About $100. See, he won't give me no more credit, but I can't blame him much. After all every man's got'a look after his own."(Whooly)

"Well now Whooly I've always found Pervice to be a reasonable man. I think maybe if you offered to hire out one of your boys to him that might work out."(Doc). "Well now I talked to him about that Doc and he said if he needed any help he'd let me know. No, but I've a little money though."(Wholly). (He got $10 from Matt earlier that morning.). "Well you'd jist give him ah little bit ya know, so how much ya got Whooly?"(Festus). "I got $10!" "Well ya got $20 now!" "Oh now Festus you work hard for yer money,

---

94 Ibid.

specially that gold piece."(Wholly). "Aw my foot! Ah paint'n ah little ole barn like at, why shoot I painted that in less an ah day! I didn't even hardly git up ah sweat, an when ole Oley saw that, he said that he never saw ah barn git painted so fast!"(Festus). "Festus! Hush up! Whooly, just wait a minute. Mr. Pervice has always been a reasonable man. Why don't you try being the same way!"(Doc). "See ya directly Whooly!"(Festus)

Ps. 72.13: He has pity on the weak and the needy, and saves the lives of the needy.

---

47. Red Paint on a Gold Coin[95]: Whooly was arrested and jailed under the suspicion of killing a man he was playing poker with the night before: **"Mathew, this here dead man is one ah them fellers in the poker game with Whooly an Tanner,"** says Festus. "You sure?"(Matt). "Course I'm sure, look here at this wad ah money, and how about this, that there is my ten dollar gold piece I give ta Whooly!"(Festus). "Festus, you got any idea how many ten dollar gold pieces there are around in Kansas?"(Matt). "There's mighty few of em speckled with red like this here one!"(Festus). "What do you mean?"(Matt). "Well that there's red paint off'n ole Oley Goodson's barn when I painted it last week! Looks

---

95 Ibid.

like ole Whooly was ah tell'n the truth now don't it? Cause that there is the gold piece I gave him!"(Festus)

Prov. 12.17: He who speaks the truth gives honest evidence, but a false witness utters deceit.

Hos. 4.4: Yet let no one contend, and let none accuse, for with you is my contention, O priest.

—⁂—

48. 'Money Bags' Festus[96]: A hot summer day in Dodge City, Kansas and Festus is sitting in a chair outside the Marshal's office talking to Doc: **"Doc, how many steps do ya think they is betwixt here an the Long Branch?"**(Festus). "I haven't the faintest idea and I don't care!"(Doc). "How much do ya figger ah feller would sweat betwixt here and there on ah day as hot as this here'n is?" "DO WHAT?"(Doc). "Sweat! I'll tell ya I'm so dry I'm about to spit my second bale ah cotton!"(Festus)

Two young farmers, Chad & Orb, come drawing up in a wagon during their conversation: **"Howdy Chad, Orb! Hot enough fer ya? Ya fellas better git outa the sun there before ya gits melted down right where yer ah set'n at!"**(Festus). "Come on over to the Long Branch and we'll buy you and Doc a

---

96 Various episodes with Festus Haggen from Season 12: 1966-67 through Season 20, 1974-75.

cold beer!"(Chad) "By jingles we'll do it cept I'm buy'n the beer!"(Festus). "All right we'll let you!"(Chad)

Chad & Orb drive on down the street to the Long Branch and Festus gets out of his chair heads off that way talking to himself and walks into the Long Branch with Doc: **"I'll be Bill look what I went an did…I offered to buy a beer fer two of the finest fellers that's hit Dodge in ah long spell an I jist ain't got the price of it!"**(Festus)

"Howdy Orb, Chad! Me an ole Doc is fix'n ta buy ya them cold beers!"(Festus). **"Oh shut your trap moneybags, I'll buy the beers! It'll be two Kitty!"**(Doc) **"Miss Kitty if ya know'd what I found about this ole scudder Doc!"**(Festus). **"Just give him his beer maybe he'll keep his mouth shut, and put two more beers up for Chad and Orb!"**(Doc)

Ecc. 1.4-9: A generation goes, and a generation comes, but the earth remains forever. The sun rises and the sun goes down, and hastens to the place where it rises. The wind blows to the south, and goes round to the north; round and round goes the wind, and on its circuits the wind returns. All streams run to the sea, but the sea is not full; the place where the streams flow, there they flow again. All things are full of weariness, a man cannot utter it; the eye is not satisfied with seeing, nor the ear filled with hearing. What has been is what will be, and what has been done is what will be done; and there is nothing new under the sun.

Prov. 25.21: If your enemy is hungry, give him bread to eat; and if he is thirsty, give him water to drink.

---

49. Good Teamwork[97]: "Where'd those shots come from?"(Matt) "Off thata way Mathew, over in the woods an most come from over yonder. Maybe ah bull's run into ah cabin er somebody's night camp!"(Festus). "Let's go! It's that Billy Boles killer outlaw we've been looking for!"(Matt). "Sure save us ah lot ah fuss and bother if we shot him right here an now Mathew instead ah taken him back to Hays!"(Festus). "A lot of people would like to see him back there Festus! Circle around over there behind the cabin and cover me from there!"(Matt)

Festus comes up from behind Boles: **"Hold it there Boles an drop yer gun or I'll be ah drop'n ya right there in yer tracks!"(Festus)**

1Thes. 5.3: When people say, "There is peace and security," then sudden destruction will come upon them as travail comes upon a woman with child, and there will be no escape.

---

97 1966-67: Season 12, Series No. 424, No. 15 in season, written by Calvin Clements, Jr.

50. Festus Builds the Gallows[98]: "Mathew ya sure ya don't want ah cup ah coffee?"(Festus). "No I don't want any Festus."(Matt). "Why don't ya jist go on over to the Long Branch fer ah spell an I'll look after things here!"(Festus). "Well all right maybe I will. You see if the gallows is done?"(Matt). "Ya jist another nail er two an it'll be did! I'll tell ya this hang'n thing won't be over too soon to suit me an I'll say Amen to that Boyles hang'n!"(Festus). "See you later Festus!"(Matt)

Is. 66.16: For by fire will the Lord execute judgment, and by his sword, upon all flesh; and those slain by the Lord shall be many.

Mrs. Boles came into town and to the jail to see her husband with a plan to break him out, but her plan was foiled and he was hung: **"Miss Boles?"(Festus). "I come to see my husband if that's all right."(Mrs. Boles). "Now he's been ah ache'n fer ya. Remember the same rules as before. Keep away from them cell bars!"(Festus)**

Prov. 12.20: Deceit is in the heart of those who devise evil, but those who plan good have joy.

---

98 Ibid.

"Festus, the gallows ready?"(Matt). "We're all set Mathew!" "Good!"(Matt). "Well what about Mrs. Boles?"(Festus). "I'll take care of her!" Be sure to do what I told you!"(Matt). "I'll do er Mathew! An when this hang'n is all over an done, I'll take the gallows down fer ya!"(Festus)

Est. 5.13-14: "Yet all this does me no good, so long as I see Mordacai the Jew sitting at the king's gate." Then his wife Zeresh and all his friends said to him, "Let a gallows fifty cubits high be made and in the morning tell the king to have Mordecai hanged upon it; then go merrily with the king to the dinner." This counsel pleased Haman, and he had the gallows made.

---

51. Festus Tears Down the Gallows[99]: Doc, Matt, and Festus are walking down the street heading for the Long Branch and Doc starts the conversation: **"Now listen, when are you going to take that gallows down Matt?"(Doc). "The sooner the better! What about it Festus?"(Matt). "Well I was fix'n ta git to it Mathew. How much ya fix'n ta pay me?"(Festus). "PAY YOU?"(Doc)**

"I thought you were volunteering your services on this!"(Matt). "Well fiddle, I put it up fer noth'n, but the taken it down? Ya know taken it down it's ah whole heap ah difference!"(Festus). "How much you figuring you'll

---
99 Ibid.

get paid for this?"(Matt). "Well it orta be worth ah beer er two!"(Festus). "BLACKMAIL!"(Doc). "Doc it's worth it! All right Festus you take that down and I'll buy you all the beer you can drink!"(Matt)

"Oh! Before er after?"(Festus). "After what!"(Doc). "Before I take er down er after I take er down? Now if I was ta have that beer after I took er down ya see I could'a worked up ah good deal ah thirst an I could drink quite ah passel ah beer, but if I was ta drink the beer before I was ta take er down, chances are I'd be relaxed an I could drink quit ah bit!"(Festus). "Good grief, I don't understand you one bit!"(Doc) "Aw fergit it, I'll splain it ta Miss Kitty an she would understand!"(Festus)

Job 12.14: "If he tears down, none can rebuild; if he shuts a man in, none can open."

Prov. 31.6-7: Give strong drink to him who is perishing, and wine to those in bitter distress; Let them drink and forget their poverty, and remember their misery no more.

52. Wonders Never Cease[100]: A freeloader by the name of O'Quillian came to Dodge and upset the daily routine of the town: **"Much obliged fer the beer Miss Kitty. Say**

---
100 1968-69: Season 14, Series No. 469, No. 6 in season, written by Ron Bishop.

Mathew is it true I been hear'n that O'Quillian went ta work at the stables?"(Festus). "It's true Festus."(Matt). "You got'a know he's got old Louie doing the work for him!"(Doc). "LOUIE?"(Kitty). "He hasn't had a drink in a week!"(Doc). "It must be true what they say, wonders will never cease to happen!"(Kitty). "In fact Miss Kitty, Blacksmith Hank says he ain't never had so much time on his hands in 30 years, an that jist proves what I said! Clear as crischal!"(Festus). "What did you ever say that was clear as 'crischal'," asks Doc. "Well about that ole O'Quillian fella, I said that he was shore different an he was ah bound ta make some changes here in Dodge!"(Festus). "You mean he actually works? Is that what you said?"(Doc)

Prov. 12.14: From the fruit of his words a man is satisfied with good, and the work of a man's hand comes back to him.

Neh. 4.6: So we built the wall; and all the wall was joined together to half its height. For the people had a mind to work.

—⸎—

53. Weatherman Festus[101]: "What are you doing!"(Doc) "I'm fix'n ta go crawdaddy fish'n!"(Festus). "It's too windy!"(Doc). "Well that's all you know!"(Festus). "Well you don't have to have a great intellect to know the wind's

---
101 1968-69: Season 14, Series No. 469, No. 6 in season, written by Ron Bishop.

blowing outside!"(Doc). "It ain't gonna be if I stop it!"(Festus). "Stop the wind?"(Doc). "Course!"(Festus). "How are you going to stop the wind?"(Doc). "Well, see this little feller outside this here 'barometry' house right here? That's bad weather, an this here little girl, when she's outside now that's good weather. Now if I was ta go an shove that little feller back in under the roof ah that little house, there ain't gonna be no more wind an bad weather! Don't ya see?" (Festus). "Festus, you give me a headache!"(Doc)

Ps. 55.8: I would haste to find me a shelter from the raging wind and tempest.

Jn. 3.8: "The wind blows where it wills, and you hear the sound of it, but you do not know whence it comes or whither it goes, so it is with everyone who is born of the Spirit."

---

54. Doc's Upstanding Patient[102]: "Now let me tell you Festus, I've treated an awful lot of carbuncles in my life, but it's been a long time since I've been called to help a man that's clean laid out on his backside!"(Doc). "Ah there ya go agin make'n fun ah me!"(Festus). "No I'm not!" "Ya are too! Yer jist"....(Festus). "I'm am not! I wouldn't

---

102 1968-69: Season 14, Series No. 476, No. 13 in season, written by Calvin Clements, Sr.

think of making fun of a fine upstanding citizen like you! HA!....Upstanding! I'll tell you that's funny!"(Doc). "Hee, hee, hee! There ya go agin, ya jist can't keep from rag'n on me!"(Festus). "It's funny! Upstanding! Don't you see? Upstanding is about all you're going to be doing for the next two weeks after I give you this scalpel cut in your rear end!"(Doc). "Hush, jist hush now! Ya know someth'n? It's agin yer 'hypocraticle' oath ta keep spout'n all the time ah make'n jokes about one of yer patient's misery!"(Festus). "Patient?"(Doc). "Ya, patient!"(Festus). "Yer no patient, yer a charity case!"(Doc). "Wait jist ah minute! What'd I tell ya when Mathew got back from Topeka an paid me fer my deputy'n an I'd pay ya? Did I say that er didn't I?"(Festus). "That's what you said, but you'll figure some way to get out of it!"(Doc). "Oh I ain't gonna do no such ah thing!"

"I'll tell you ole pinch-penny, if yer so blamed worried about that money, I'll go borry 50 cents from Miss Kitty right now an pay ya!"(Festus). "50 CENTS! Now as I recall this incident you came up to my office because you were in terrible pain, so I dropped everything and I performed a very, very delicate surgery on you, and now you tell me that you think that 50 cents is proper payment?"(Doc). "Oh ya jist help me git set up here in this cot so'est I can beat ya at checkers!"(Festus)

"I'll say one thing, you sure are one rip-snorting thing of the law and order here in Dodge City!"(Doc). "There ya go agin, ya jist can't quit! Why don't ya give them flappety jaws oh yers ah little rest, an me too! I swear ya jist make me sick!"(Festus). "You have to admit you're not exactly a fit candidate for a posse right now!"(Doc). "Doc, if yer gonna keep rag'n me, I ain't gonna play checkers with ya!"(Festus). "Oh go on and make your move and hush up!"(Doc)

Ecc. 9.16: But I say that wisdom is better than might, though the poor man's wisdom is despised, and his words are not heeded.

Prov. 17.5: He who mocks the poor insults his Maker; he who is glad at calamity will not go unpunished.

Jer. 20.7: O Lord, thou hast deceived me, and I was deceived; thou art stronger than I, and thou hast prevailed. I have become a laughingstock all the day; everyone mocks me.

---

55. Louie Pheeters is Innocent![103]: Festus, in a moment of compassion, released accused murderer Louie, the town drunk, from jail so he could go talk to two young men, the Rucker boys, who he thought were witnesses to the killing he was accused of while he was in a drunken stupor, and the two boys admitted they were the ones that did the accidental crime. Festus

---

103 1969-70: Season 15, Series No. 498, No. 9 in season, written by Joy Dexter.

paces the floor at the Marshal's office while telling Matt of his concern and worry that Louie may not ever come back, but Louie does come back and he has the two young men and their father with him:

"Howdy Louie," says a very excited Festus. "Thank you Festus," says Louie. "Ah fiddle, I know'd you'd come back. Like I jist got done tell'n Mathew, I said ole Louie, he ain't never been on time fer noth'n."(Festus)

Prov. 28.13: He who conceals his transgressions will not prosper, but he who confesses and forsakes them will obtain mercy.

Js. 5.16: Therefore confess your sins to one another, and pray for one another that you may be healed. The prayer of a righteous man has great power in its effects.

---

56. Who Is Thomas Jefferson?[104] "Well now, what's them cockle-burrs do'n in town? Whoa up there ah minute! Elbert Moses what er ya do'n back here in Dodge, fix'n ta stir up some kind of ah rookus are ya," asks Festus. "Me and my cousin come in ta town ta celebrate Thomas Jefferson's birthday!" "Who's Thomas Jefferson anyway," Festus asks. "Ya orta go ta school and do some learn'n cause ya

---

[104] 1969-70: Season 15, Series No. 497, No. 8 in season, written by Calvin Clements, Sr.

don't know who he is," says Elbert. "Ah it don't make no matter ta me," says Festus. "OK! Who is he," asks Elbert. "Who's what?"(Festus). "Thomas Jefferson!"(Elbert). "Well I know'd who he is! I jist bet'n you mutton heads er ask'n cause ya don't know yer ownselfs!"(Festus). "No ya don't! Thomas Jefferson was the third Prezeedent of these United States," says Elbert. "Course he was! Yer ah say'n like you's the onlyest ones in the world that know'd who he was! Pffftt!"(Festus)

Ecc. 10.12: The words of a wise man's mouth win him favor, but the lips of a fool consume him.

Prov. 15.2: The tongue of the wise dispenses knowledge, but the mouths of fools pour out folly.

Prov. 14.6: A scoffer seeks wisdom in vain, but knowledge is easy for a man of understanding.

---

57. 100th Meridian[105]: Festus ran into an old retired sea captain on the street in Dodge: **"Say! You got'a an ole bald noggen'd, runny mouthed spawler'd shank friend with ah patch over one eye ah go'n by the name of Watney?"**(Festus). "Well, yes I do. How did you know that?"(Captain). "Well of

---

[105] 1970-71: Season 16, Series No. 531, No. 16 in season, written by Wm. Kelley.

course I know'd it! After listen'n ta his slack-jaw all week, I feel like I know bout twice as much bout you as I'll ever have any need fer!"(Festus). "You must have him locked up?"(Captain). "Locked? Oh no, me an ole Watney got quainted whilest build'n fence out ta widow Birny's place. See, her place is right next door ta your'n!"(Festus)

"WAIT! WAIT! Wait a minute! Mr. Watney is supposed to be building us a ranch house!"(Captain). "Well that's what he says, but ah fact is, there ain't no part of a ranch house he can build or I'm a two-footed angle worm! What it is, is ah big ole tall scraggelty look'n may-pole kind of ah thing!"(Festus). "HA! He's built himself a tall ship's mast, just like he said he would, right at the 100th meridian!"(Captain)

"Oh no! No it's built right on the ground!"(Festus). "The 100th meridian is an imaginary line that you can't see! That's why I came here in the first place! Always said I'd build my ranch house on the 100th meridian, as far as I could get from both shores!"(Captain). "If'n ya can't see it, how in tarnation do ya know it's there, an what's that got ta do with shores?"(Festus). "It's 100 degrees of longitude west and it's built right through the front porch equidistant from the Atlantic and Pacific oceans, and now the quarterdeck is northeast quarter west!"(Captain). "Pffttt! Don't make no more sense than ah mule's tail on its nose!"(Festus)

Jer. 29.5: Build houses and live in them; plant gardens and eat their produce.

Prov. 9.1: Wisdom has built her house, she has set up her seven pillars.

Prov. 14.1: Wisdom builds her house, but folly with her own hands tears it down.

Prov. 24.3: By wisdom a house is built, and by understanding it is established.

58. Festus' Worstest Best Friend[106]: Festus recognizes a long-lost childhood best friend, Cleavus Lucas, who wanders into the Long Branch to buy a drink. He recently killed an old prospector in a fit of rage over the old man calling him 'son', even though the old man befriended him and gave him food and drink when he was in dire need. Cleavus has a terrible bad temper brought on by his hatred of his bringing-up and childhood memories, and he has a chip on his shoulder against anyone who reminds him of his circumstances in life. He took a bag of gold dust from the body of the dead prospector and buried him on his claim. Feeling rich in his new-found gold mine and personal wealth Cleavus rides for the nearest town which happens to be Dodge City:

---

106 1970-71: Season 16, Series No. 536, No. 21 in season, written by Richard Scott.

"Cleavus is that you?"(Festus). "Well if it ain't Festus Haggen!"(Cleavus). "Cleavus you ole rat skinner you! Yer ah sight fer ah feller's sore eyeballs! What in tarnation er ya do'n here in Dodge?"(Festus). "I just ah drift'n an the like. Are you ah Marshal?(Cleavus). "Nah jist ah Deputy." "Looks like ya did yerself right proud Festus." "Oh it ain't noth'n! Oh! Excuse me Cleavus, this here is Miss Kitty, Miss Kitty I want ya ta meet my bestest friend Cleavus Lucas. We know'd each other since we was knee-high to ah grassityhopper! Cleavus, Miss Kitty owns this here Long Branch saloon!"(Festus). "Well now Festus she's a right pretty lady. Pleased ta meet ya Miss Kitty!" "Pleased to meet you Cleavus! Any friend of Festus is a friend of mine. Welcome to Dodge!"(Kitty)

"Cleavus, ya recollect that ole cabin my daddy built out yonder on the Pickanaw River?"(Festus). "I'll never ferget that!"(Cleavus). "You come'n ta live with us that one winter...the times we had! Ah, them was good times Cleavus!"(Festus). "NO they weren't Festus!"(Cleavus). "Now we had us a heap ah good times there Cleavus! Plenty ah good vitals ta eat, big, wide open prairie ta hunt on, an creeks ta fish in, ah home an folks that took care of us. Why we jist....!"(Festus). "NO! You did, NOT ME! My folks jist passed me off ta live with ya. I could never get on good with my folks! Never did! But that don't mean no never mind now! The time I was born, I lived like ah mangy dog! Folks step'n up ta ah grow'd man, say'n 'Boy' an treat'n him like trash cause he didn't git right on when he's ah holler'd at. Well that dog won't hunt no more! NO SIREE, that ole dog won't hunt no more, cause I got me ah plan! Cleavus Lucas has got his self ah plan start'n tomorrow! Yes sir!" "Pffttt.. ha!"(Festus)

"What's so funny," asks Cleavus. "Well it ain't funny maybe, jist like it always was, yer favright say'n 'onlyest wait til tomorree someth'ns bound ta hap'n tomorree', they ain't no good tadays accord'n ta ya! What's this here grandyest plan of yer'n?"(Festus). "Well, how would ah body like me go about file'n ah claim right here in Dodge City?"(Cleavus). "I reckon ya jist go on over yonder ta the govermunt land office an talk ta them fellers, but Cleavus folks ah been poke'n all over this part of the county, an they's ah right smarter'n you an I never have seen nobody come up with ah pinch ah gold!"(Festus). Festus, my mind's made up!"(Cleavus). "Ya always did have ah hard set'n mind Cleavus! Good night!"(Festus). "Good night Festus, an tomorrow I'm ask'n Miss Kitty ta dinner an I'll be ah ask'n her ta marry me!"(Cleavus). "Pffttt! Ya, and it snows down yonder there where the Devil lives, you ole scudder you!"(Festus). "Tomorrow Festus, tomorrow...I have ah plan!"(Cleavus)

Gal. 6.3: If someone thinks he is something when he is really nothing, he is only deceiving himself.

Prov. 6.30-31: Do not men despise a thief if he steals to satisfy his appetite when he is hungry? And if he is caught, he will pay sevenfold; he will give all the goods of his house.

Prov. 14.7: Leave the presence of a fool, for there you do not meet words of knowledge.

Festus discovers Cleavus' secret after he kidnaps Kitty, and Festus goes after him at the gold mine to rescue Kitty and arrest Cleavus. Cleavus bushwhacks Festus and attempts to kill him by pushing him into a cavernous hole inside the mine, but then he has second thoughts and saves him by extending the stock of his shotgun so Festus can grab on and climb out. In the strain and scuffle the shotgun goes off and fatally wounds Cleavus. Cleavus speaks his dying words while Festus cradles his friend in his arms:

"Festus, I'll make it up to ya tomorrow……tomorrow I'll be rich you'll see…. I've got ah plan fer…………. tomorrow… Cleavus dies in Festus' arms, and Festus says, **"Tomorrow Cleavus…tomorrow."**

Prov. 26.11-12: Like a dog that returns to his vomit is a fool that repeats his folly. Do you see a man who is wise in his own eyes? There is more hope for a fool than for him.

Prov. 11.3: The integrity of the upright guides them, but the crookedness of the treacherous destroys them.

Prov. 19.21: Many are the plans in the mind of a man, but it is the purpose of the Lord that will be established.

Prov. 17.9: He who forgives an offense seeks love, but he who repeats a matter alienates a friend.

2Sam. 22.47-49: "The Lord lives; and blessed be my rock, and exalted be my God, the rock of my salvation, the God who gave me vengeance and brought down peoples under me, who brought me out from my enemies; thou didst exalt me above my adversaries, thou didst deliver me from men of violence.

59. Festus' Patent[107]: Festus has come up with an idea he wants to patent and is explaining it to Matt and along comes Doc Chapman:

"Well don't ya think at there is ah smart idea Mathew? Wouldn't that jist be the very thing? You never had hear'd no idea as good as this one!"(Festus). "I hate to throw cold water on your idea, but……..,"(Matt). "Wait, wait! DOCTOR! Doc could you come in here ah minute and tell Mathew this here is ah good idea that I got? Jist tell him

---

107 1971-72: Season 17, Series No. 544, No. 5 in season, written by Jack Miller.

it's ah good idea!" "Festus! What's a good idea?" "Well, I had me that chicken with the runny sauce all over it at Delmonico's fer supper last night an figgered that's what brung on this here dream that give me this good idea that I'm fix'n ta git one of them things from Warshington that guarantees ya that nobody can't step up behind yer back an steal yer idea!"(Festus). "That's it?"(Dr. Chapman)

"Yeah!"(Festus). "You got an idea you want to get a patent on?" "Ya, wooden trains!"(Festus). "Wooden trains?" "Yeah, trains made outa wood, don't ya see?"(Festus). "I didn't quite catch on either doctor."(Matt). "Well don't ya see, wood trains could float right across the rivers!"(Festus). "Wooden trains floating across the river?"(Dr. Chapman). "Ya, that's it!" "And you could put paddles on the drive shafts to help drive the trains across the river and alls right!"(Dr. Chapman). "Well you blame shore could! Doctor, that's ah very golly ole make-em! That's ah good idea! Mathew? See what I told ya?"(Festus). "Yeah, yeah that's right Festus. Congratulations doctor, you catch on to things fast! It takes some people quite awhile!"(Matt)

"Festus, they is just one little change I'd make if I were you."(Dr. Chapman). "Huh? What's that doctor?"(Festus). "Wouldn't it be cheaper to make the rails out of wood, then float on top of the water, and let the trains go across the rivers that way?"(Dr. Chapman). "NO! NO! Now doctor that wouldn't work! Don't ya see, ya laid them wood rails across the river an they'd be all wobblety an catywompus and you couldn't never hold no steady!"(Festus). "All right, but what if you was to take these big posts and drive them down into the river bed and then attach the rails onto the posts. That wouldn't be wobblety then would it?"(Dr. Chapman). "Well it blame shore wouldn't! I believe that'd work. That'd hold em steady as ah rock!"(Festus). "I've even got a name for that kinda rails!"(Dr. Chapman). "Yeah, what's that?"(Festus). "A BRIDGE! Heh, heh, heh!"

Prov. 14.23: In all toil there is profit, but mere talk tends only to want.

---

60. Two Quacks in Dodge[108]: Festus is lamenting to Kitty about how Doc pesters him: **"He'll call me a mutton head and then he'll build up ta where I ain't got enough sense ta fill a thimble, and then he'll start ta insult me. I can hear him do'n it!"** Just then Doc walks into the Long Branch: **"I think a deputy Marshal here in the saloon this early in the morning drinking hard liquor!"(Doc)**

"All right you ornery ole scudder jist never you mind ah call'n me ah mutton head and stuff like at!"(Festus). "I haven't called you anything yet!"(Doc). "The way it peers ta me ah doctor is supposed ta be patient with his patients suspect'n ta have patience!"(Festus). "Can you translate that for me

---

108 1969-70: Season 15, Series No. 507, No. 18 in season, written by Benny Rubin.

Kitty?"(Doc). "I think he has a toothache Doc."(Kitty). "Well for heaven's sake all you got'a do is go up in my office and wait for me like you always do, but you know as well as I do that your toothache will completely disappear the very second you hear my footsteps on the stairs!" "Aw fiddle!"(Festus)

"Now I want to talk to you about something Deputy, you got a badge. Now you know how Matt and I feel about Quacks coming into this town, well right at this very minute one of 'em has parked his rig down at the livery stable and he's registered over at the Dodge House, now why do you allow a thing like that? Well why do you?" "Well, maybe Dodge is git'n big enough fer two Quacks!"(Festus). "YOU, YOU GO…..don't you get smart with me! Here you take this medical bag and you get up to my office and you wait for me!"(Doc). "Where ya go'n?"(Festus). "None of your business! I don't know which tooth is bothering you, but it certainly is not a **WISDOM** tooth!"(Doc). "Pfft!"(Festus)

Prov. 18.17: He who states his case first seems right, until the other comes and examines him.

Prov: 15.1: A soft answer turns away wrath, but a harsh word stirs up anger.

Ecc. 6.11: The more words, the more vanity, and what is man the better?

61. The Long Branch Rooster[109]: Doc discovers the alleged Quack is his old medical schoolmate friend Herman Schultz, and Herman demonstrates his hypnotic abilities, and Doc asks him to pull a prank on Festus up at his office. Festus is hypnotized and Doc pulls his tooth without him suffering pain. Then Doc asks Herman to set up a public prank on Festus: **"I wouldn't want to miss this opportunity for anything in the world Herman. Now while you've got him like this, is it possible to make him think he's an animal or anything like that?"** "Oh yes, a chicken or a duck, or a rooster perhaps?"(Herman). **"ROOSTER! That's it!"**(Doc). "All right, very simple. He doesn't even have to be mesmerized."(Herman). **"What do you mean?"**(Doc). "Well when we put someone to sleep you can tell them what to do and after the wake up they do it!"(Herman)

"All right, I'm going over to the Long Branch and you give me a couple of minutes, and you make Festus a rooster, and bring him over there!"(Doc). "I'll see you soon."(Herman). Festus wakes up when Herman snaps his fingers: **"Oh, Doc leave did he Dr. Schultz?"**(Festus). "Yes he will meet us at the Long Branch."(Herman). "Now you will go to the Long Branch and you will walk in like you are a rooster, a very big and proud rooster that feels like crowing! Crow five times!"(Herman)

---

109 Ibid.

Festus walks into the Long Branch and starts crowing and flapping his wings. He jumps up on a table and stands on his tip-toes and starts crowing and flapping his wings with great gusto, and all the Long Branch patrons break into a laughing uproar:

Kitty asks, "Festus what on earth has gotten into you?" "Well Miss Kitty, they's times when ah feller jist has to do what he feels like and I jist felt like crow'n and flapp'n my wings! What's so bad about that?"(Festus). "You're acting like a jackass, that's what!"(Kitty). "Now Dr. Schultz,... Herman! "Put Festus back the way he was! I liked him better that way," says Doc.

Prov. 1.26: I also will laugh at your calamity; I will mock when panic strikes you.

Prov. 14.13: Even in laughter the heart is sad, and the end of joy is grief.

Prov. 15.33: The fear of the Lord is instruction in wisdom, and humility goes before honor.

Prov. 22.4: The reward for humility and fear of the Lord is riches and honor and life.

62. Trail Boss Festus[110]: Festus rides his mule, Ruth, into Dodge in a big hurry to make an announcement about a cattleman trail boss who wants to hire some men to herd cattle and bring them into Dodge for sale to a broker who is waiting to receive them and load them on the train to go to market:

"Hush up, Hush up everybody, HUSH, HUSH everybody. HUSH NOW! We're fix'n ta ride outa here directly and we're go'n ta ride out ah here like we had brains enough ta know which way we're go'n! Now Mr. Cumberlidge, he put me in charge ta fetch him back some good men and that's what I aim ta do. I don't want no polyfox'n around! No who-haw'n, and who-raw'n an trouble make'n!"

Some fellow in the crowd of anxious men yells out: "Shut your mouth Festus, and let's get going!" "Who said that! Which one of ya said that! Somebody wants ta git his ears pinched off,....oops, Hi Mathew! We jist fix'n ta ride over by yer office there ta let ya know we're ah head'n out!"(Festus). "Ya, well you know what to tell Cumberlak," says Matt. "Ya, ya, jist move the herd jist south of the Abe Johnson place and hold em there!"(Festus). "That's right, and when he gets here he is to see me and we'll make arrangements to bring his boys into town!"(Matt). "Jist like it's rit across't my eye balls Mathew! You ain't got noth'n ta fret about!"(Festus). "All right Festus take care of yourself!"(Matt). "Jist like a

---

110 1967-68: Season 13, Series No. 440, No. 2 in season, written by Clyde Ware.

scuttle in a coal bin Mathew! This here's go'n ta sharpen up my teeth. I'll guarantee ya that! OK! Everybody foller me…..YO..Oh, Ohh!"(Festus)

Prov. 10.8: Sensible people accept good advice. People who talk foolishly will come to ruin.

Prov. 12.14: From the fruit of his words a man is satisfied with good, and the work of a man's hand comes back to him.

---

63. Everybody Welcome[111]: Dodge is having a barn dance and Festus is in charge of setting up the livery stables for it: Festus comes stomping across the street and yells out to Burk and Louie:

"You knuckle heads quite flap'n yer jaws an put the banner up there over the door like I told ya!" (Festus). Louie says, "I'm just trying to tell you this here banner is…" The banner is upside down: **Festus yells back, "I don't care! Louie, I got more important'ner things ta do ta git ready fer this party than ta stand here an try to tell ya how ta do real simple things!"(Festus). Burk yells back at Festus, "If you'll just listen, we're trying to tell you….." "BURK! Now I ain't go'n ta stand here and argue with ya! Now I want ya ta cinch it RIGHT THERE where I tell'd ya to, and do it RIGHT NOW," yells Festus.**

---

111 .1967-68: Season 13, Series No. 442, No. 4 in season, written by Calvin Clements, Sr,

Watching from across the street, Doc says to Matt, "Now that don't surprise me one bit!" "Hi Doc, Mathew," says Festus. "Festus, that's not right!"(Doc). "What's not right?"(Festus). "When are you going to learn to read?"(Doc). "Now I jist barely said howdy and all ready yer rag'n on me!"(Festus). "When are you go'n to learn to read and write anyway?"(Doc). "All right Mr. Smart-Alecky, high who-haw, I'm jist started to learn!"(Festus). "That's kind of hard to believe!"(Doc). Festus turns and points to the sign: "Well, I'll jist show ya! (He reads the sign to Doc).'**BARN PARTY EVERYBODY WELCOME**'!"(Festus). Doc bends down and leans his head upside-down and looks at the sign over the barn door: "**Well I'll be dog-gone'd, He's right, that's what it says! I guess I was mistaken! Here all the time I thought you were backward! Now I know you are UPSIDE-DOWN AND BACKWORD!**"(Doc)

Prov. 8.5: O simple ones, learn prudence; O foolish men, pay attention.

Prov. 8.10: Take my instruction instead of silver, and knowledge rather than choice gold.

---

64. Abelia[112]: While making his night-rounds in Dodge, Festus interrupts a robbery in Doc's office. A wanted man took a woman (Abelia) hostage to show him where he could steal laudanum

---

112 1968-69: Season 14, Series No. 471, No. 8 in season, written by Calvin Clements, Sr.

for his injured partner. Festus got a glimpse of the woman before he was knocked out. He woke up and tracked down the thieves at the woman's farmhouse and in a gunfight he killed them. He recognized the woman from the incident in Doc's office.

Festus has compassion for the widow lady and her two children, and understanding her plight, he has no plan to take her in to jail for thievery. He has spent the better part of a day helping Abelia, the widow lady with two young children (a girl and boy) at her farm and he is taken with her looks and friendliness, and the children, but now it is near the end of the day and he must make tracks for Dodge:

Abelia says, "Sure you won't stay for supper Mr. Haggen?" "I'd sure like to maam, but I reckon I better git on an try ta catch up ta Mathew on the trail," Festus says. The little girl says, "You mean you ain't coming back to spark ma?" "Well!"....(Festus). "Aw, that ole cow is out again why don't you kids go see if you can't get her tied up," says Abelia. "Good bye Festus," say the kids. "My kids kinda speak up, they ain't too much for talk'n polite," says Abelia. "Aw, they wasn't unpolite a' tall maam, fact is you must be mighty proud of them two young'ns."(Festus). "Yes, I am very proud of them."(Abelia)

"Well, I'm sure plum pleasurable ta meet up with ya, I jist wish that we could'a met up under more pleasuresome times, but then Dodge City, it ain't so far from here to where you won't maybe be see'n me ride by. I could even git close't enough ta where I'd be down here to ya."(Festus). "Well, you come that close might's well come close enough ta holler ah hello." (Abelia). "Heh, heh, that's kinda what I had in my head."(Festus). "Fact is Sundays I always cook up more dinner than me and the kids can eat, just in case we have a neighbor pass'n by."(Abelia). "Well, I reckon I can keep that one in mind all right, well, I think I reckon I better be git'n along. Take care of them young'ns now and take good care of yerself, hear me?"(Festus). "Bye!"(Abelia). "Bye, bye you young'ns! Take care of yer ma now!"(Festus). "Bye Mr. Haggen!

Festus rides off down the road kicking up dust: **"Isn't he a nice man ma,"** says the little girl. **"He sure is darl'n, a very special man."**(Abelia). **"You said that about our Pa. Will Mr. Haggen ever be back ma,"** say the children. **"I don't know children,....I don't know."**

Ps. 112.5: It is well with the man who deals generously and lends, who conducts his affairs with justice.

1Thes. 2.7: But we were gentle among you, like a nurse taking care of her children.

Deut. 10.19: Love the sojourner therefore; for you were sojourners in the land of Egypt.

Mic. 6.8: "He has showed you, O man, what is good; and what does the Lord require of you but to do justice, and to love mercy, and to walk humbly with your God."

Prov. 31.26: She opens her mouth with wisdom, and the teaching of kindness is on her tongue.

65. A Little Peace & Quiet[113]: In the Long Branch sitting around a table are Matt, Doc, Festus, and Kitty:

"Festus, you got to help me by staying here and looking after things," says Matt. "Well, Newly can do that Mathew, now yer gunn'a need somebody,"....Kitty brings four cups of coffee on a tray and sits down **"much obliged Miss Kitty! Like I's say'n Mathew, now Newly can look after Dodge, besides you know what times has changed out yonder in that town of Hilt! Why it's worser than Dodge ever was in its worstest,"** says Festus.

"Uh-huh, you know what he's working up to Matt? He wants to go along with you!"(Doc). "Well course I do! How the tarnation do we know who their figger'n to send out yonder to Hilt ta help him?"(Festus). "Matt didn't you say whoever would be helping, would be staying on for awhile

---

113 1973-74: Season 19, Series No. 604, No. 17 in season, written by Paul Savage.

after you quiet things down?"(Kitty). "That's what the telegram said Kitty."(Matt). "Well, then why don't you take Festus with you?"(Kitty). "I think that's a great idea! Matt, why don't you do that, then we can get a little peace and quiet around here!"(Doc). "All right ya blamed ole scudder. If I was ta ever leave Dodge, you'd be miserabler'n ah flea bit ole hound dog with a rhoommy-tickie hind leg! Besides that you wouldn't find nobody that'd put up with yer blamed pickety-pickety hooplaw!"(Festus). "Oh, yes I'm going to miss this already!"(Matt). "You be careful, ya hear me Mathew?"(Festus). "See you Festus!"(Matt). "Well after all this time you'd think the good byes would get easier, but they don't!"(Kitty). "See you in a couple of weeks!"(Matt)

Prov. 18.19: A brother helped is like a strong city, but quarreling is like the bars of a castle.

Prov. 11.3: The integrity of the upright guides them, but the crookedness of the treacherous destroys them.

Prov. 19.21: Many are the plans in the mind of a man, but it is the purpose of the Lord that will be established.

66. Doc is Alive & Well[114]: Doc and Newly are in Doc's buggy and coming back into Dodge after a medical visit in the

---

114 1973-74: Season 19, Series No. 598, No. 11 in season, written by Calvin Clements, Sr.

hill country where Doc was accidentally shot when Festus and Newly were attempting to defend him from an angry crowd of hill country folks. Doc's life is saved by the surgery performed on him by Newly:

"Now Newly, just let me off right here. I want to walk up the street to my office from here," says Doc. "You're going to get all the exercise you need just climbing those stairs," Newly says. "Well all right, maybe you're right, take me up there! You have no idea how good this feels, just to look up and down the street of Dodge."(Doc). "Yes I do Doc." "Whoa, here we are!"(Doc). You bet Doc, just a second I'll give you a hand."(Newly). "All right."(Doc)

Festus walks across the street right by Doc while humming a tune without even looking at him:

"Pfferr, pfferr, howdy Doc," says Festus. "Wait a minute! Just a minute here! Come back here," yells Doc. "What's the matter!"(Festus). "Is that all you got to say to me is 'Howdy Doc' and Pfferr, pfferr?"(Doc). "Well, what else is there ta say?"(Festus). "Well, good heavens I've been gone all this time and is that all you've got to say to me?"(Doc). "Fiddle, I ain't missed ya none! Nobody in town has I don't reckon! Everybody's still sick jist like they was when you was here doctor'n em! Pfft! Well, I can't stand around here ah jaw'n with you all day. I got more importantner things ta do an that!"(Festus). "Oh sure, I know you have, you better....,"(Doc). "Doc!" "Doc!"(Newly). "Someday I'm going to get him!"(Doc)

"Doc, I could sure use a beer, and I think you could use one too, don't you?"(Newly). "Doctor O'Brien! Since you've called me in on this consultation, it's my considered opinion that you have just prescribed for me the perfect prescription!"

Doc and Newly walk through the swinging doors of the Long Branch to a large celebration gathering of town folks for his healthy return from near death:

Kitty says, "Somebody said, 'tough old buzzard', I say more loveable!" She kisses him: "It was me that called you a 'tough old buzzard' Doc," says Matt. "WE MISSED YOU DOC," shout the crowd of townspeople. "Doc, I've been save'n a toe twinge fer ya," says Festus. "Here's to Doc's health," Kitty toasts. "A fella is gone a little while and you!" "Oh! This is a lot of nonsense," says Doc. And with that the crowd breaks out in robust laughter.

Prov. 17.17: A friend loves at all times, and a brother is born for adversity.

Jn. 15.13: "Greater love has no man than this, that a man lay down his life for his friends."

67. Doc's Homecoming[115]: Doc Adams was gone to Baltimore for several months to receive further medical training. He has returned to Dodge City in the early evening without telling anyone and was in his office when Festus came stomping up the stairs and through the door looking for Dr. Chapman (Doc Adams' stand-in) Doc is in the back room of his office:

"Doctor! Doctor Chapman! We were ah wonder'n.... WHAT? Doc?" "Festus, how are ya?" "Doc you ole scudder you, what er ya do'n here?" "What am I doing? Why good heavens, this happens to be my office!" "Aw, it shore is good ta have ya back in Dodge!"(Festus)

Festus wrestles him and gives him a big hug: **"What are you doing? STOP IT! Now what's the matter with you!"**(Doc). "It seems like you been gone ah 100 years! Why didn't ya let us know you was come'n?"(Festus). "Well, just for this very reason! I didn't want all of this fussing around. I didn't want that!"(Doc). "Oh golly Bill, Doc, I missed ya someth'n fierce!"(Festus). "You did?"(Doc). "You betcha!"(Festus). "Well I don't know why. Good heavens you had Dr. Chapman here, and he's a fine doctor!"(Doc). "Well, he's ah good enough feller, but it jist wasn't the same without you Doc!"(Festus). "Oh, you mean he charged you!" "All right! There ya go agin! All that learn'n yer supposed to have got in

---
115 Various episodes with Festus Haggen from Season 12: 1966-67 through Season 20, 1974-75.

Baltymore ain't changed ya one little smidgen! Yer still orneryner an meaner an ah teased rattler snake, an yer jist plain lucky that I didn't take ya fer ah thief an shoot ya in the head, the way ya come ah slip'n in ta town!" (Festus). "I didn't come slipping into town!" "Well ya did too!" "I did not!" "Ya didn't even stop ta say howdy to Mathew or Miss Kitty!" (Festus). "I was getting ready to do that when you came slipping in here!"(Doc). "Oh, ya was?"(Festus). "Sure!"(Doc). "All right, I'll tell ya what I'm fix'n ta do!"(Festus). "WHAT!"(Doc). "I'm fix'n ta take ya over yonder an buy ya the tallerest beer they is in Dodge!"(Festus). "HOLD ON! WAIT! YOU are going to buy ME a beer?"(Doc). "I'm buy'n! Well, course if'n ya don't want it!" (Festus) "WAIT a minute! I want it, and I'm going to get it! You're not going to change your mind? You're not going to get out of this!"(Doc)

They go down to the Long Branch where Matt, Newly and everybody is congregated for the evening and Doc and Festus walk through the swinging doors:

"Hey lookie here who's come back!"(Festus). "DOC!"(Kitty). "I guess ya don't mind Miss Kitty hug'n ya!"(Festus). "When did you get back Doc?"(Kitty). "Oh a little while ago."(Doc). "You planning on staying or are you going to run out on us?"(Kitty). "Oh no, I'm going to stay! I'm not going anywhere!"(Doc). "Doc, you'll never know how much we've missed you."(Kitty). "Well I'm sure glad to know that, because I sure missed you! Where's Matt?"(Doc). And Festus says, "He's down ta the office! Let's all go down yonder ta the office an surprise ah bunch off'n him!"

Lk. 15.22-24: "But the father said to his servants, 'Bring quickly the best robe, and put it on him; and put a ring on his hand, and shoes on his feet; and bring the fatted calf and kill it, and let us eat and make merry; for this my son was dead, and is alive again; he was lost, and is found.' And they began to make merry."

Prov. 3.3-4: Let not loyalty and faithfulness forsake you; bind them about your neck, write them on the tablet of your heart. So you will find favor and good repute in the sight of God and man.

Prov. 18.24: There are friends who pretend to be friends, but there is a friend who sticks closer than a brother.

68. Crawdads at Midnight[115.1]**:** Festus came up to Doc's office late at night with a burlap bag full of crayfish and said to Doc: **"Eve'n Doc, I jist got back from that ole Rookster's place!" "Is that right," says Doc. "Yea, ya know Judd an Annie an Wonder that young Indian boy, have jist patched**

115.1 1967-68: Season 13, Series No. 452, No. 14 in season, written by Mary Worrell & Wm. Blinn.

up and dolled up that place that ya couldn't hardly recognize it a'tall, an that Wonder he might jist stick with em an go ta school fer learn'n. I been help'n em by dig'n ditches all day!"(Festus). "NO! I don't think you ought to go there at all," says Doc. "Well, why!"(Festus). "Because they're newlyweds and they'd kinda like to be left alone," says Doc. "Well, not when they's ah dig'n no ditches they don't! Me an Jud been dig'n ah ditch all day from the pond over ta the vegetable garden!"(Festus). "What's in the sack," asks Doc. "All right smart-aleck, what's in the sack?"(Festus). "Crawdads you found in the Rooker's pond! That's what's in the sack, but the question is, what in thunder are you doing up here this time of night in my office?"(Doc). "I want ta tell ya about that! Now ya see my mouth ah jist been water'n all day someth'n fierce fer some fried crawdads! Well, now when I got back ta town, ya see Mathew he done asleep in the jail house, an I's down ta Delmonico's an it's done closed, an whether ta wake up Ma Smalley's at this hour, why I....."(Festus). "You just thought you'd bring them up to ole Doc's and he'd say go ahead and fix em right here!"(Doc). "Ya, well much obliged Doc! I ain't gonna bother ya none, know'n how ya feel about it, but have ya got ah big pot someplace where I can start ta boil em?" (Festus). "Yer not going to do it!"(Doc). "Well, ya gotta boil em before ya shuck em, then ya fry em! Don't ya see?"(Festus). "Yer not going to boil or shuck, or fry any crawdads up here! NOW GET OUT'A HERE!"(Doc). "WHY NOT!"(Festus). "Because this happens to be a doctor's office, that's why! It is where I treat the sick and I'm not going to have it smelling like a fish market! Now get them out of here!"(Doc). "All right, sore head, I'm go'n!"

Festus picked up the burlap by the wrong end and the crawdads spilled out all over the floor: **"LOOK WHAT YA DONE, here pick those up! You've spilled them, now pick them up, every last one, pick them up!"**(Doc). "Jist hold yer taters, I'm pick'n em up! I'll pick ever last one of em up, an I'll take em with me an I'll fry em, an I'll eat em all! An I'll invite Miss Kitty and Mathew an we's go'n to eat ever last one of em, an we ain't go'n ta bother you no more Mr. Squeemy!"(Festus). "Well that's perfectly all right if you want to be selfish about it!"(Doc). "SELFISH?"(Festus). "Sure, you got enough crawdads there for a whole army!"(Doc). "You want to eat them?"(Festus). "It just so happens I kind of like them!"(Doc). "Now, jist tonight ya told me they was creepy crawdads an you didn't like em!"(Festus). "I didn't say I didn't like to eat them! I think they're delicious! I don't know anything that I like better than fried crawdads, unless maybe it's a nice big platter of boiled calves brains and horseradish! Now you talk about a delicacy! Yes! You see, just give me a platter of boiled calves brains and horseradish and.....!" (Doc). Festus got up off of the floor with his hand over his mouth and went out the door and down the steps coughing and choking, and left his bag of crawdads behind.

Is. 1.19: If you are willing and obedient, you shall eat the good of the land.

Prov. 22.9: He who has a bountiful eye will be blessed, for he shares his bread with the poor.

---

69. Festus Go'n In'ta Business[116]: Festus, Doc, Matt, and Kitty are sitting around a table in the Long Branch and Festus strikes up a conversation about all the new businesses coming into Dodge lately: **"Ya know ah lot ah new businesses is come'n inta town in the last couple ah years,"** says Festus. **"Yes, there are new ones coming into Dodge everyday,"** Kitty says. **"Well its about time I put some do'n inta all the think'n I been do'n,"** says Festus. **"What think'n is that Festus,"** asks Matt. **"Well, about me go'n inta business fer myself! (Festus). "BUSINESS? Business for YOU,"** retorts Doc. **"YES! BUSIINESS, smart aleck! Us Haggens been in the business business fer many and ah many ah years!"(Festus). "Oh! You been in the business business have you now! Well then, how do you figure profit and loss! Now how do you do that?"(Doc). "I ain't go'n inta business fer no loss ya ninny! I'll tell ya this, ah feller buys someth'n fer one penny, then he goes ta work an sells it fer two pennies, that there's ah profit! Now, what figure'n does that there take!(Festus)**

---

116 1967-68: Season 13, Series No. 447, No. 9 in season, written by Calvin Clements, Sr.

Prov. 14.23: In all toil there is profit, but mere talk tends only to want.

―⁂―

70. Festus Crosses the Cimarron[117]: Matt, Festus, Doc, and Kitty are in the Long Branch sitting around a table, and Festus just got a free beer from Kitty and she asked him how he crossed the Cimarron River: **"Festus I want to hear how the cow crossed the river? How did you ever think of that?"(Kitty). "Oh, fiddle Miss Kitty that there wasn't my idea, that there was my gram paw Hog Haggen's idea!"(Festus). "Now wait a minute Festus how'd your grandpa Haggen get in this," Matt asks. "Well, ya see Mathew the way it was is gram paw Hog Haggen was the onlyest one us Haggens that could read read'n an I recollect when I was no bigger'n ah tater bug gram paw use to read us young'ns these here stories out'a the Bible. An there was this here one story bout this here feller in Egypt that was escape'n from the Ferrys!"(Festus). "Wait a minute, hold on…oh you mean the Pharaoh!"(Doc). "Ya! One ah them fellers, an directly they come run'n up ta this here great big ole wide crick!"(Festus). "It wasn't a crick, it was a sea, the Red Sea!"(Doc). "Well, when this here Mose feller….."(Festus). "His name was Moses!"(Doc). "Well, when he seen the sea, ya see, well he went ta work an**

---

117 1972-73: Season 18, Series No. 570, No. 7 in season, written by Charles J. Stone.

scrunched up his eyeballs an he commenced ta git bear'n down on at that crick, directly why he balled up his fists like that, and then he slammed em out sideways like at... and he said OPEN YERSELF UP WATERS!"(Festus). "And the waters parted, right?"(Kitty). "Oh, course they did! Jist like they wasn't even there a'tall in the first place!"(Festus). "Just a minute now, just a minute! Are you going to sit there and tell me that you went into some kind of a rooster dance and parted the waters of the Cimarron River?"(Doc). "Golly-Bill, no Doc! Course I done a few little gee-jaws at the very begin'n!"(Festus). "Well, what in thunder is all this silly story you're telling about then?"(Doc). "Well, when I seen them fellers ah nip'n at my boot heels bout ta catch up ta me, I seen this ole heifer an I jist collar'd er an rode er right on through the river! Don't ya see?"(Festus). "This is the most ridiculous and inane story that I think that I have ever heard in my life. Festus, why in thunder don't you learn to read so that when you want to tell something you would have read it and you could get the facts and tell them straight!"(Doc). "Doc, I told ya 100 dozen times, when ya start ta read read'n, how do ya know that the feller that wrote the read'n, wrote the read'n right!"(Festus)

Ex. 14.21-22: Then Moses stretched out his hand over the sea; and the Lord drove the sea back by a strong east wind all night, and made the sea dry land, and the waters were divided. And the people of Israel went into the midst of the sea on dry ground, the waters being a wall to them on their right and on their left.

—⸺

71. Water Witch'n[117.1]: "I saw water witched the many the many the time Mathew! I recollect when I was jist knee high to ah beetle bug my aunt Tory Heep went out an cut herself ah apple wood fork an she went ah walk'n out on ah piece ah ground that didn't show no more sign ah water than the back ah my hand! Well, she started ah sashshay'n around an directly it started ta dip'n an ah dart'n an ah pull'n an ah gee'n an ah haw'n, an purty soon that fork jist pulled right down ta the ground, an they was water jist like that!" (Festus).

Prov. 11.25: A liberal man will be enriched, and one who waters will himself be watered.

Prov. 25.25: Like cold water to a thirsty soul, so is good news from a far country.

117.1 1967-68: Season 13, Series No. 462, No. 24 in season, written by Harry Kronman.

Post Script

Marshal Matt Dillon had a total of five deputies over two decades in the *Gunsmoke* series, and Curtis remains the best known for his role as Festus. He played his role for eleven years, and 239 episodes (the longest) as the colorful, 'lovable' deputy.

In 1981 Ken Curtis was inducted into the Western Performers Hall of Fame at the National Cowboy & Western Heritage Museum in Oklahoma City, Oklahoma. He died in his sleep of a heart attack in Fresno, California on 29 April 1991 at the age of 74 years. He was cremated and his ashes were scattered in the Colorado flatlands. A statue of Curtis as the Festus character may be found at 430 Pollasky Avenue in Clovis, California.[118]

As situations arose in his life, Festus' emotions, much like our own, were like a roller coaster. Throughout his years as deputy U.S. Marshal he often exhibited anger, a quick temper and frustration, but his moral compass throughout his life pointed

---

[118] Wikipedia.com: Available under the Creative Commons Attribution-Share Alike License. 2016.

to kindness, tender-heartedness, and love for his friends and neighbors, and those in need.

Gal. 6.7-10

"Do not be deceived; God is not mocked, for whatever a man sows, that he will also reap. For he who sows to his own flesh will from the flesh reap corruption; but he who sows to the Spirit will from the Spirit reap eternal life. And let us not grow weary in well-doing, for in due season we shall reap, if we do not lose heart. So then, as we have the opportunity, let us do good to all men, and especially to those who are of the household of faith."[119]

---

119 The Holy Bible, Old & New Testaments: Revised Standard Version.

Printed in Great Britain
by Amazon

Oriental
Giant

Rodrigo Vargas

China – The Oriental Giant

China – The Oriental Giant

Copyright © 2011 - 2015 - Rodrigo Vargas
All rights reserved.

Note: Much care and attention, as well as best practices were used in the production of this book, however, may have occurred typing errors, mistakes of figures, or other issues that generate doubts; in all cases we kindly ask you to contact us through the website www.WithinManagement.com, and we will try to solve the issue or refer the matter. In addition to that, your suggestions for improvements are also very welcome.

Cataloging in Publication
Catalog Card Made by the Author

HC	Vargas, Rodrigo
94	China: The Oriental Giant / Rodrigo Vargas. Self-Published by the Author, printed by
-1085	CreateSpace, through the print on demand system, from 2012.
V297	102 p.; il.; 15.24 x 22.86 cm (6" x 9")
2012	

ISBN-10: 1503110370
ISBN-13: 978-1503110373

1. Economy. 2. Macro Economics. 3. China. I. Title

DDC: 339   UDC: 338

About the Author

Experienced plant manager, consultant and author of business and management books, Rodrigo Vargas has over 17 years of experience in the industrial environment, and over 13 years of experience dedicated to management positions in the automotive and electro-electronic industry, with professional experience in Europe, Asia and Latin America. Rodrigo is a Brazilian Mechanical Engineer, post graduated in Business Management and Mechanical Maintenance Engineering. He was certified Lean Six Sigma Black Belt, Lead Auditor of Quality System Management, and Practitioner in Neurolinguistic. Rodrigo was a Financial Mathematics teacher and has completed the Teaching Course specialization in Getulio Vargas Foundation. Rodrigo is the founder and editor of the industrial management portal GestaoIndustrial.com (in Portuguese), and the international management blog WithinManagement.com

Summary

ABOUT THE AUTHOR 7

SUMMARY 9

FOREWORD 11

MY IMPRESSIONS 13

GOVERNMENT 19

    GOVERNMENT DATA 20

    ADMINISTRATIVE DIVISIONS: 21

GEOGRAPHY 23

PEOPLE 25

    RELIGIONS IN CHINA 26

    LITERACY 27

    POPULATION 28

    POPULATION GROWTH RATE 29

    AGE STRUCTURE 30

    LIFE EXPECTANCY AT BIRTH 31

    URBANIZATION 32

ECONOMY 33

    GROSS DOMESTIC PRODUCT (GDP) 34

    GDP REAL GROWTH RATE 35

INVESTMENT	36
INFLATION RATE	37
EXCHANGE RATE	38
TRADE BALANCE	39
ELECTRICITY BALANCE	40
ENERGY MATRIX	41

SHANGHAI 43

SCENES FROM CHINA 59

END OF TRIP 81

Foreword

I have stayed a month in China, in 2010, and, based on this awesome experience, I have decided to put together my impression, some information and some images that I believe are interesting, and that can give a good overview of some interesting aspects about China.

One of the main objectives is to give a macro perspective about the strong Chinese economy, and to show some key success indicators related to that. For a better comprehension of the numbers about China, I have made a comparison with USA, the biggest economy in the world, and with Brazil, one of the biggest emerging markets. I have updated all the metrics in 2015 with the best information available that I could find, and that are, basically, from data provided by the Central Intelligence Agency (CIA) and by the World Bank.

I would say that this book is like a travel album with some very interesting technical information about the economy and people. Good reading and enjoy the trip!

Rodrigo Vargas

My Impressions

I was in China during the month of April, in 2010, and had the opportunity to know some of the culture and way of life of the Chinese people. What you will read next is purely my impressions after this experience.

People - The people are very friendly. An occidental guy gets a lot of attention, anywhere in China, mainly out of the biggest cities, but that's not uncomfortable, at least I have never felt bad because of that. It is common to be greeted in the street, or approached in the supermarket, and even feels like a movie star during a visit in any typical place.

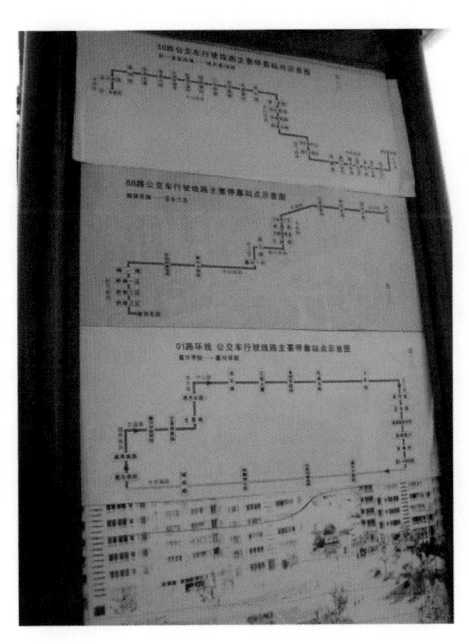

The challenge is really the language, that's tough! Because of the big difference between English and Chinese, sometimes I felt like a deaf-mute (see the bus stop totem picture). Out of Shanghai, was not easy to find someone speaking English, neither at the hotel. Only at the company I was working for, I could find some English speakers.

Another interesting point, I have never felt unsafely in China. Even walking at night, from railway station to the hotel, never had problems with regards safety.

Food – I have enjoyed the food, even though it's spicy, I had not issues with that. I did not find the food so different from what I am used to eat: rice, meat, chicken, fish, vegetables... Instead, some snacks, usually offered on streets (for example, some small animals fried) which I have tasted, are a bit different. Of course, it's an experience to prove it, but you might not like it (see the picture below).

Commerce - It's quite impressive how people buy all day long. The commerce usually opens the doors at 8:00h in the morning and goes hot until close at 22:00h (see the picture below). It is easy to understand the phenomenon of the growth of China's economy, when we realize that besides the huge export market (*since China is the world's largest exporter, representing about 27% of its GDP, Brazil exports represent approx. 11% of GDP, and USA about 10%, according to CIA estimates for 2011*), China has a huge and highly consuming domestic market. Even in the holidays they opened the commerce.

Allied with strong consumption, China has one of the highest rates of investment; and you can easily see a lot of evidences of the investment from the Government, like new roads, railways working and being built, overpasses, airports, ports, etc. According to the data from CIA for 2010, investment in China was 47.8% of GDP, while in Brazil, 18.5% of GDP, and the USA, 12.8%. Thus, with high consumption and high investment, and production following consumption, the result ends up being a high growth economy.

Industry – There is a joke that I heard from some Chinese guys that says: *If it exists, you can find it in China.* Now a day, Chinese people have a lot of opportunities, much more than years ago, to choose for a job in the industry. I was told by the local administrator in the Company, that it was not difficult people left the job because of another offer. It is intense the industry activity, but, at the same time, they face an energy issue, and they have to respect some limits using the electricity, since the balance in China is very small (see the chart).

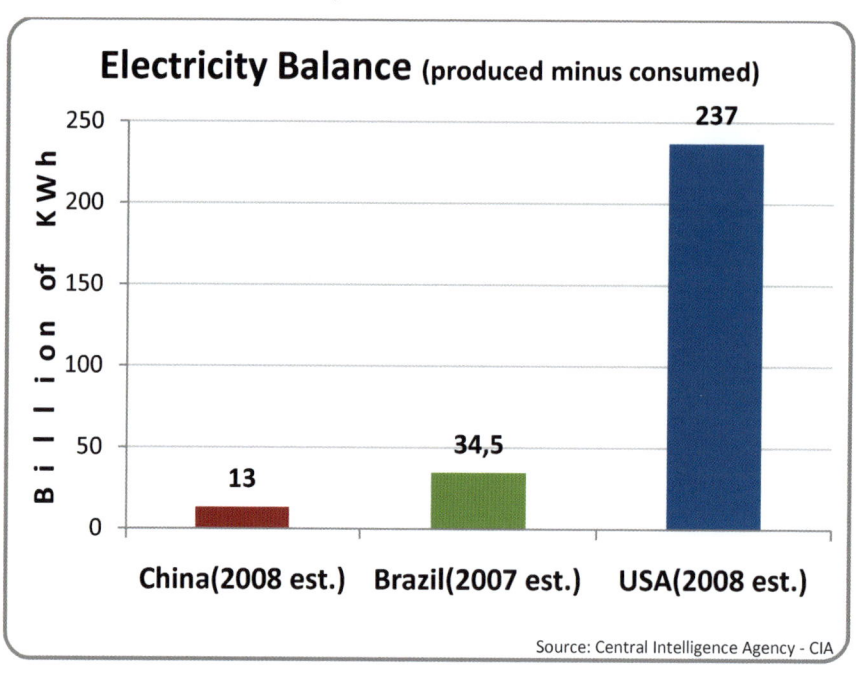

Electricity Balance (produced minus consumed)

	Billion of KWh
China (2008 est.)	13
Brazil (2007 est.)	34,5
USA (2008 est.)	237

Source: Central Intelligence Agency - CIA

According to the CIA (2013 est.), the Industry accounts for 43,9% of GDP in China, 26,9% in Brazil, and 19,5% in USA.

The low-cost labor in China (well known advantage) is tending to increase, and the middle/high cost of equipments tends to decrease. The quality of Chinese products is getting better and better, because of the use of equipments on the process, the partnership with occidental companies, and the high demand associated with the learning curve.

Despite of the electricity issue, the transportation in China works well, and the infrastructure is helpful, making Chinese suppliers reduce lead times because of good roads, rail roads, ports, airports, etc. Even though I have already heard about issues in this area, I believe that China is in a good shape. Of course, considering the high growth of the country, there is room for improvements.

My 30 days stay in China was awesome and remarkable, and left a general impression that China is a great country, culturally rich, good destiny to work, and good as well to travel.

Government

Facade Detail of the South Lake Chinese Revolution Memorial Hall in Jiaxing

Government Data

Country conventional long form: People's Republic of China (PRC)*

Country conventional short form: China

Country local long form: Zhonghua Renmin Gongheguo

Country local short form: Zhongguo

Government type: Communist State

Chief of State: Presidente Xi Jinping (since 15 November 2012), President Hu Jintao (from 15 March 2003 to 15 November 2012);

Capital: Beijing

Independence: 1 October 1949 (People's Republic of China established); notable earlier dates: 221 BC (unification under the Qin Dynasty); 1 January 1912 (Qing Dynasty replaced by the Republic of China)

National holiday: Anniversary of the founding of the People's Republic of China, 1 October (1949)

PRC flag (image above)

Administrative divisions:

a) 23 provinces (sheng, singular and plural),
b) 5 autonomous regions (zizhiqu, singular and plural)
c) 4 municipalities (shi, singular and plural).

Provinces: Anhui, Fujian, Gansu, Guangdong, Guizhou, Hainan, Hebei, Heilongjiang, Henan, Hubei, Hunan, Jiangsu, Jiangxi, Jilin, Liaoning, Qinghai, Shaanxi, Shandong, Shanxi, Sichuan, Yunnan, Zhejiang; (see note on Taiwan).

Autonomous regions: Guangxi, Nei Mongol, Ningxia, Xinjiang Uygur, Xizang (Tibet)

Municipalities: Beijing, Chongqing, Shanghai, Tianjin

Note: China considers Taiwan its 23rd province; and Hong Kong and Macau are considered special administrative regions.

Constitution: most recent promulgation 4 December 1982 with amendments in 1988, 1993, 1999, 2004

Time difference: UTC+8 (13 hours ahead of Washington, DC during Standard Time). Note: despite its size, all of China falls within one time zone; many people in Xinjiang Province observe an unofficial "Xinjiang time zone" of UTC+6, two hours behind Beijing.

REGIONS OF CHINA

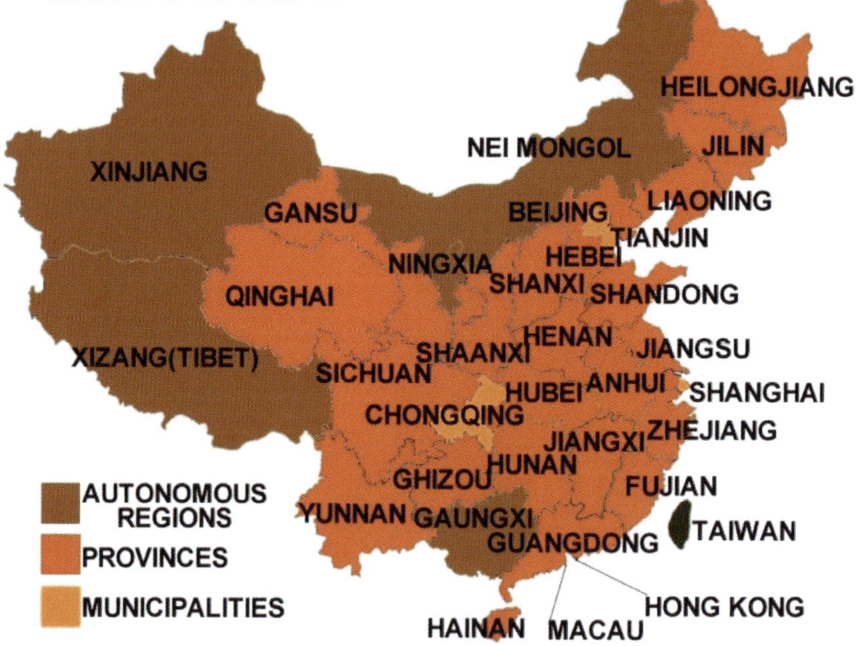

Geography

Area: 9.596.961 sq km (only smaller than Russia, Canada and US)
Natural resources: coal, iron ore, petroleum, natural gas, mercury, tin, tungsten, antimony, manganese, molybdenum, vanadium, magnetite, aluminum, lead, zinc, rare earth elements, uranium, hydropower potential (world's largest)
Climate: extremely diverse; tropical in south to subarctic in North
Terrain: mostly mountains, high plateaus, deserts in west, plains, deltas and hills in east.
Elevation extremes: highest point in Mount Everest 8.850m in the border with Nepal

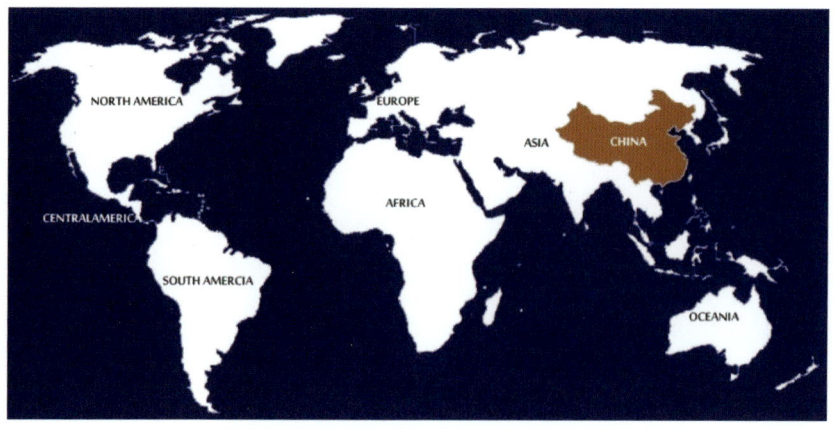

China location in the world map.

People

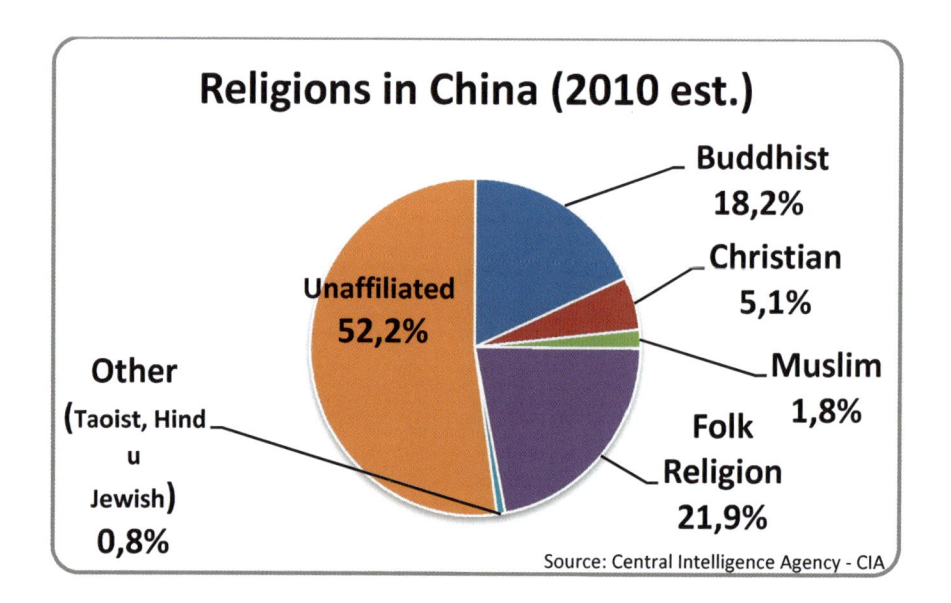

Religions in China

Religions in China (2010 est.)

- Buddhist 18,2%
- Christian 5,1%
- Muslim 1,8%
- Folk Religion 21,9%
- Unaffiliated 52,2%
- Other (Taoist, Hindu, Jewish) 0,8%

Source: Central Intelligence Agency - CIA

Religions in China: Officially atheist. Buddhist 18.2%, Christian 5.1%, Muslim 1.8%, Folk religion (ethnic or regional religious customs under the umbrella of an organized religion) 21.9%, Other (Hindu, Jewish, Taoist) <1%, Unaffiliated 52.2% (2010 est.).

Literacy

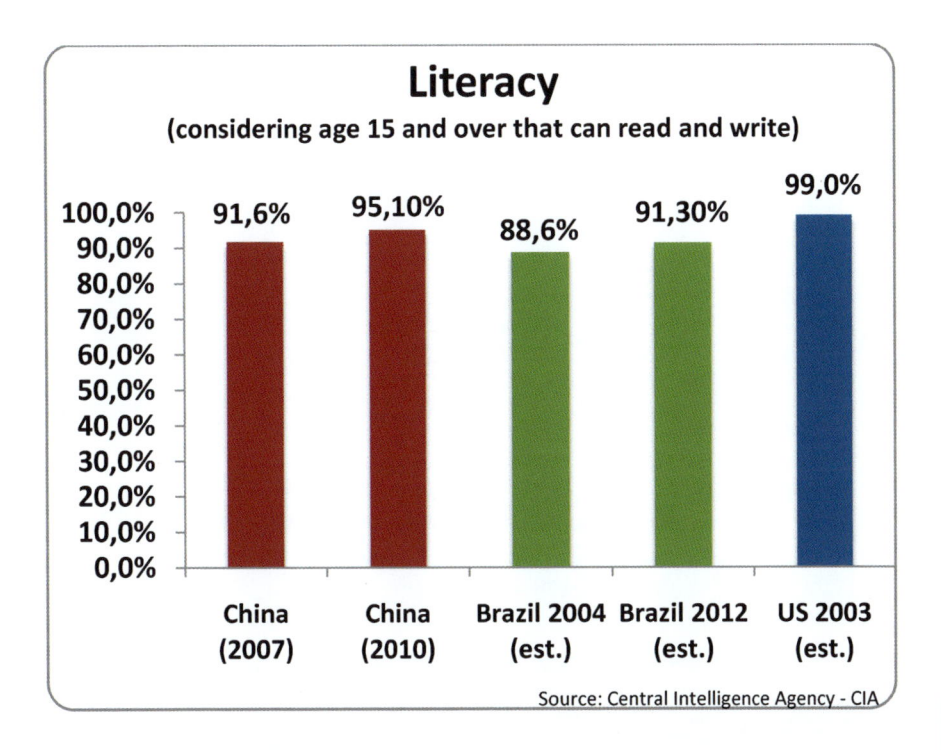

Literacy
(considering age 15 and over that can read and write)

- China (2007): 91,6%
- China (2010): 95,10%
- Brazil 2004 (est.): 88,6%
- Brazil 2012 (est.): 91,30%
- US 2003 (est.): 99,0%

Source: Central Intelligence Agency - CIA

Education expenditures: 1.9% of GDP (1999). Brazil is 5.2% of GDP (2007), US is 5.5% of GDP (2007).

Population

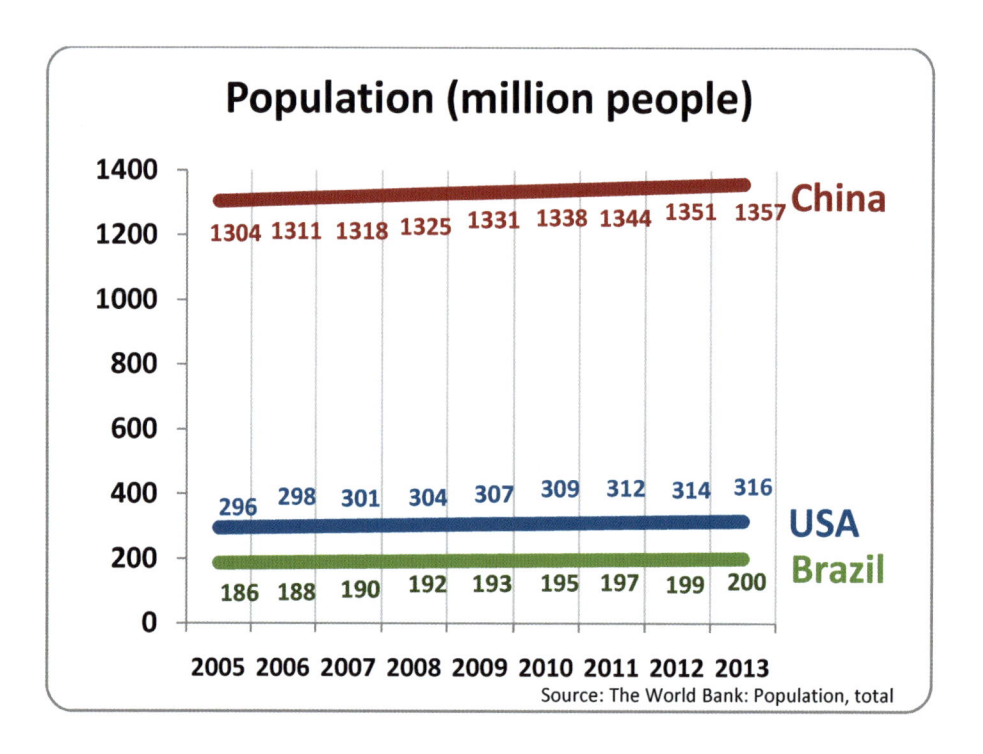

Population (million people)

Year	China	USA	Brazil
2005	1304	296	186
2006	1311	298	188
2007	1318	301	190
2008	1325	304	192
2009	1331	307	193
2010	1338	309	195
2011	1344	312	197
2012	1351	314	199
2013	1357	316	200

Source: The World Bank: Population, total

The world population in July/2010 was 6.768.181.146 of people, and China represents 19,6% of it.

Population Growth Rate

Population Growth Rate

Year	Brazil	USA	China
2005	1,2%	0,9%	0,6%
2006	1,1%	1,0%	0,6%
2007	1,0%	1,0%	0,5%
2008	0,9%	0,9%	0,5%
2009	0,9%	0,9%	0,5%
2010	0,9%	0,8%	0,5%
2011	0,9%	0,7%	0,5%
2012	0,9%	0,7%	0,5%
2013	0,9%	0,7%	0,5%

Source: The World Bank: Population Growth Rate

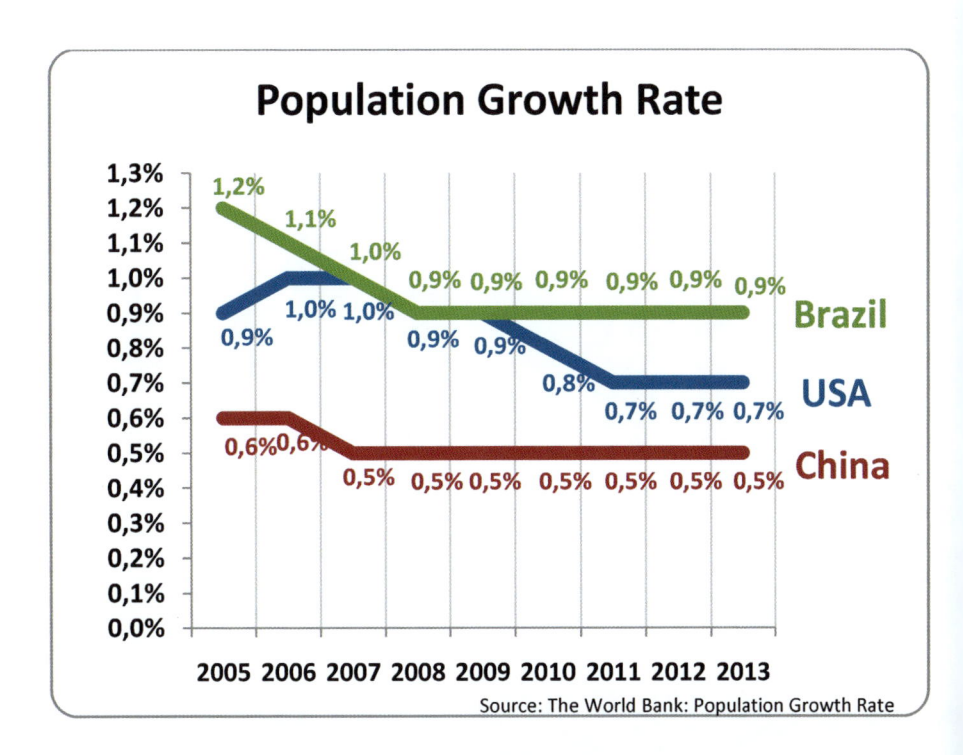

Currently China has the biggest population in the world, but a low growth rate (one of the lowest in the world).

Age Structure

Age Structure

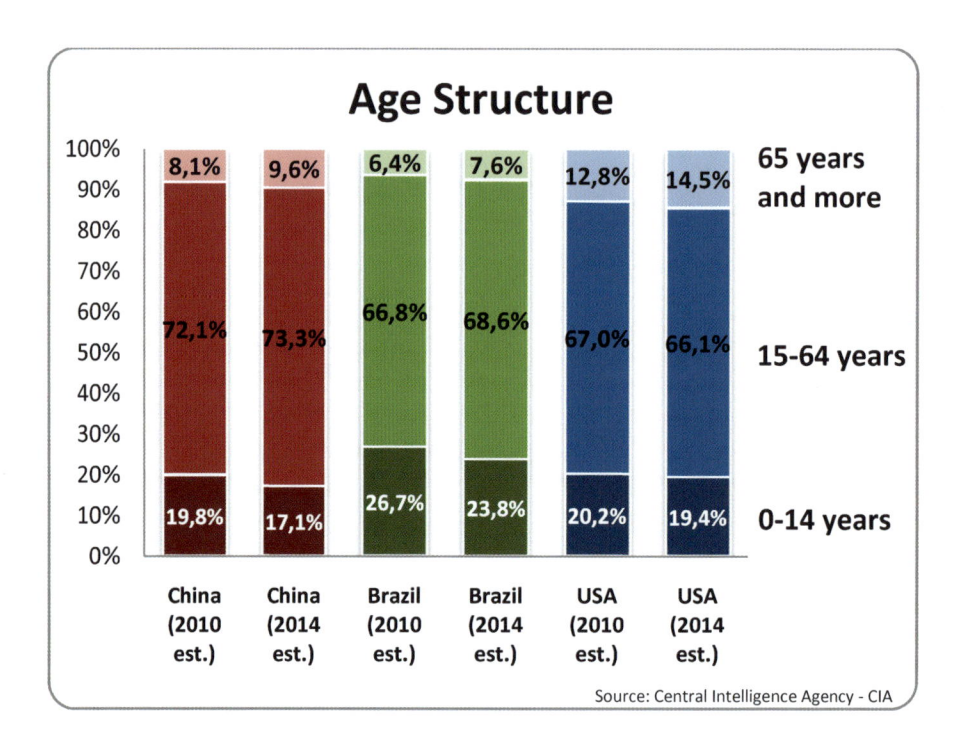

Category	China (2010 est.)	China (2014 est.)	Brazil (2010 est.)	Brazil (2014 est.)	USA (2010 est.)	USA (2014 est.)
65 years and more	8,1%	9,6%	6,4%	7,6%	12,8%	14,5%
15-64 years	72,1%	73,3%	66,8%	68,6%	67,0%	66,1%
0-14 years	19,8%	17,1%	26,7%	23,8%	20,2%	19,4%

Source: Central Intelligence Agency - CIA

It's a clear tendency of all the 3 countries analyzed here of increasing old population, which is a serious issue considering the social welfare system and public pension system, mainly in countries where the structure is not well prepared, like Brazil. Obviously, is also an issue for China, considering about 200 million retirees and 800 million people contributing to the pension fund. USA is considered a top 10 best public pension system.
See the next chart, showing the life expectance at birth for each country.

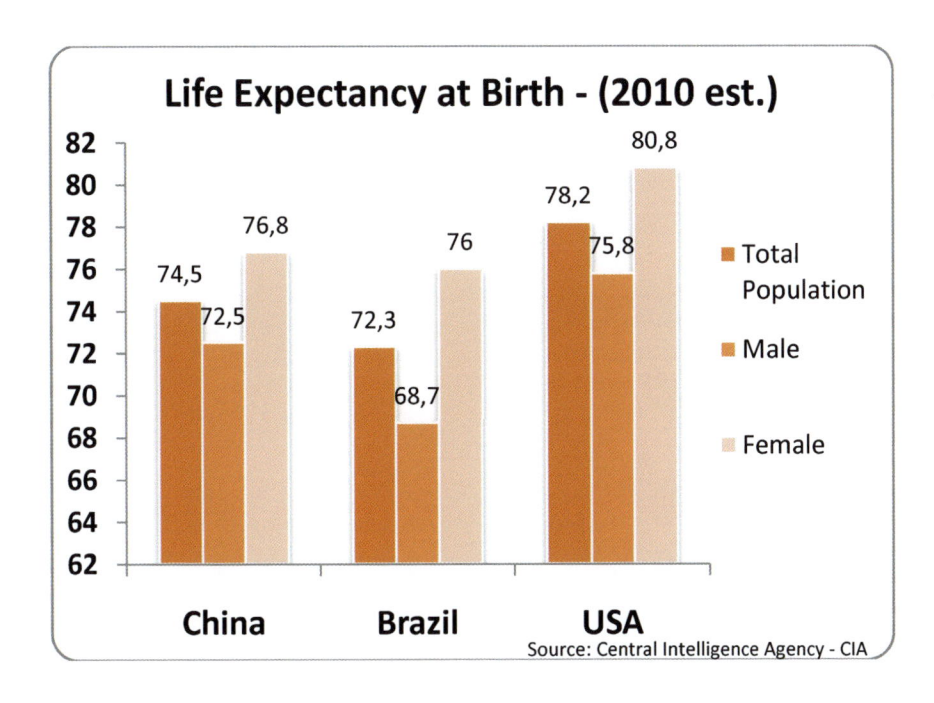

Life Expectancy at Birth

Life Expectancy at Birth - (2010 est.)

Country	Total Population	Male	Female
China	74,5	72,5	76,8
Brazil	72,3	68,7	76
USA	78,2	75,8	80,8

Source: Central Intelligence Agency - CIA

Urbanization

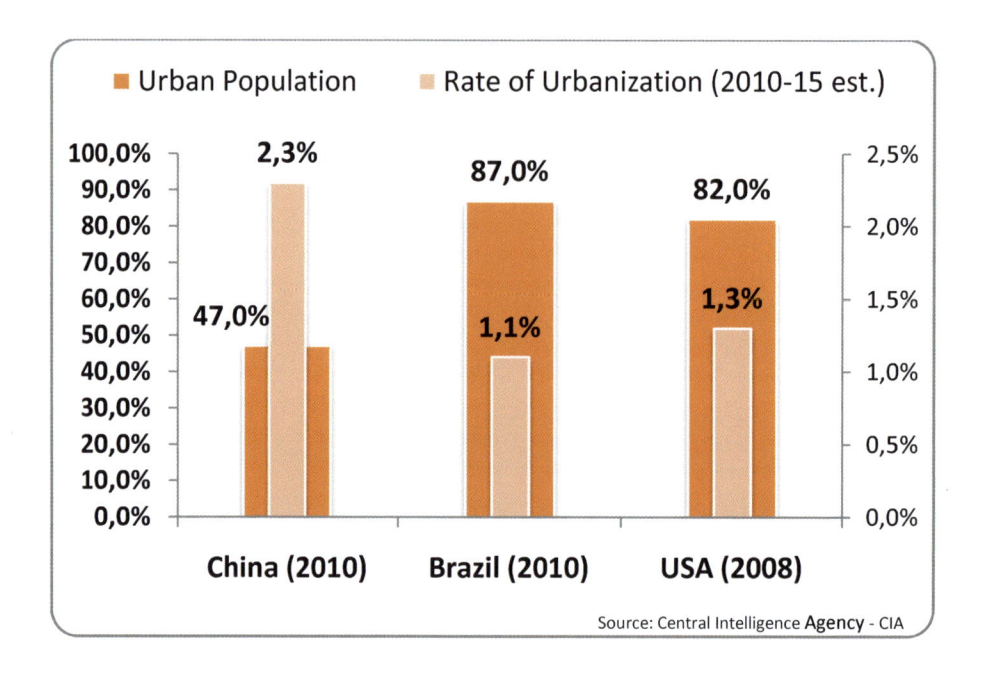

	Urban Population	Rate of Urbanization (2010-15 est.)
China (2010)	47,0%	2,3%
Brazil (2010)	87,0%	1,1%
USA (2008)	82,0%	1,3%

Source: Central Intelligence Agency - CIA

Intensive urban population growth, as well as a higher percentage of urban population can lead to greater poverty. So, it's important to open opportunities in the rural areas.

Economy

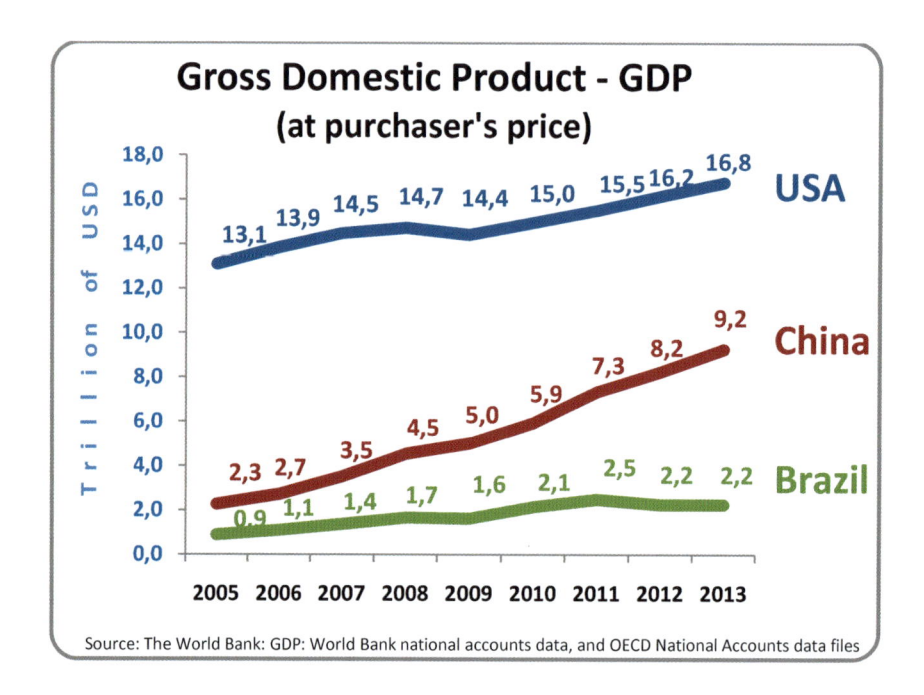

Gross Domestic Product (GDP)

Gross Domestic Product - GDP (at purchaser's price)
Trillion of USD

Year	2005	2006	2007	2008	2009	2010	2011	2012	2013
USA	13,1	13,9	14,5	14,7	14,4	15,0	15,5	16,2	16,8
China	2,3	2,7	3,5	4,5	5,0	5,9	7,3	8,2	9,2
Brazil	0,9	1,1	1,4	1,7	1,6	2,1	2,5	2,2	2,2

Source: The World Bank: GDP: World Bank national accounts data, and OECD National Accounts data files

China GDP passed Japan, becoming in 2010 the second economy in the world. Considering the current scenario, projections shows China passing USA GDP in 2028.

Note: GDP at purchaser's prices is the sum of gross value added by all resident producers in the economy plus any product taxes and minus any subsidies not included in the value of the products. It is calculated without making deductions for depreciation of fabricated assets or for depletion and degradation of natural resources. Data are in current U.S. dollars. Dollar figures for GDP are converted from domestic currencies using single year official exchange rates. For a few countries where the official exchange rate does not reflect the rate effectively applied to actual foreign exchange transactions, an alternative conversion factor is used.

GDP Real Growth Rate

GDP Real Growth Rate

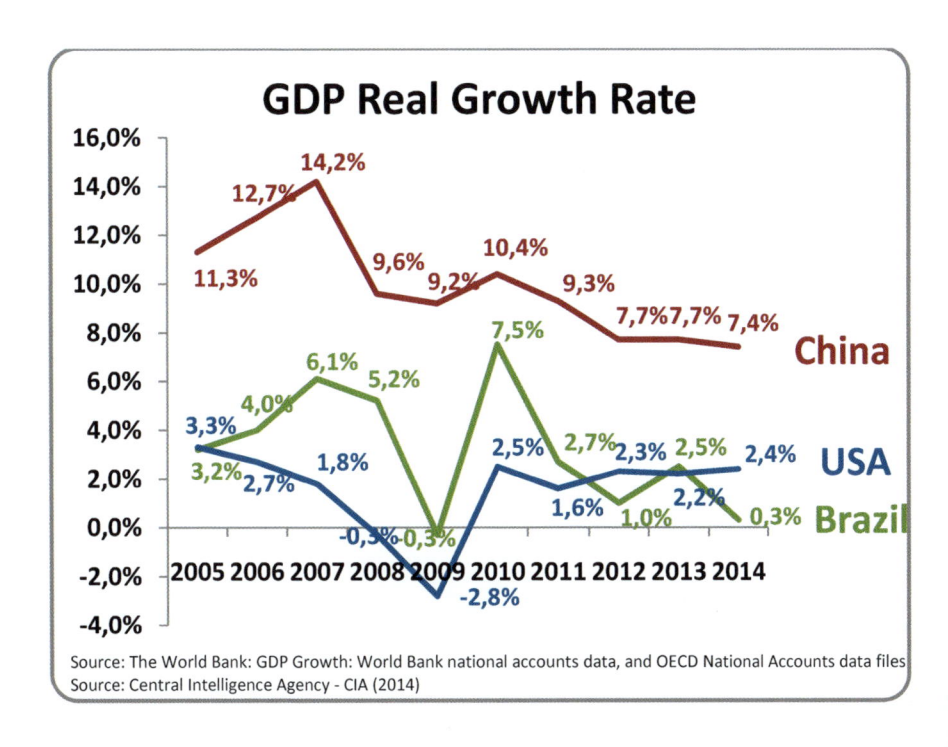

Year	China	USA	Brazil
2005	11,3%	3,3%	3,2%
2006	12,7%	2,7%	4,0%
2007	14,2%	1,8%	6,1%
2008	9,6%	-0,3%	5,2%
2009	9,2%	-2,8%	-0,5%
2010	10,4%	2,5%	7,5%
2011	9,3%	1,6%	2,7%
2012	7,7%	2,3%	1,0%
2013	7,7%	2,2%	2,5%
2014	7,4%	2,4%	0,3%

Source: The World Bank: GDP Growth: World Bank national accounts data, and OECD National Accounts data files
Source: Central Intelligence Agency - CIA (2014)

Investment

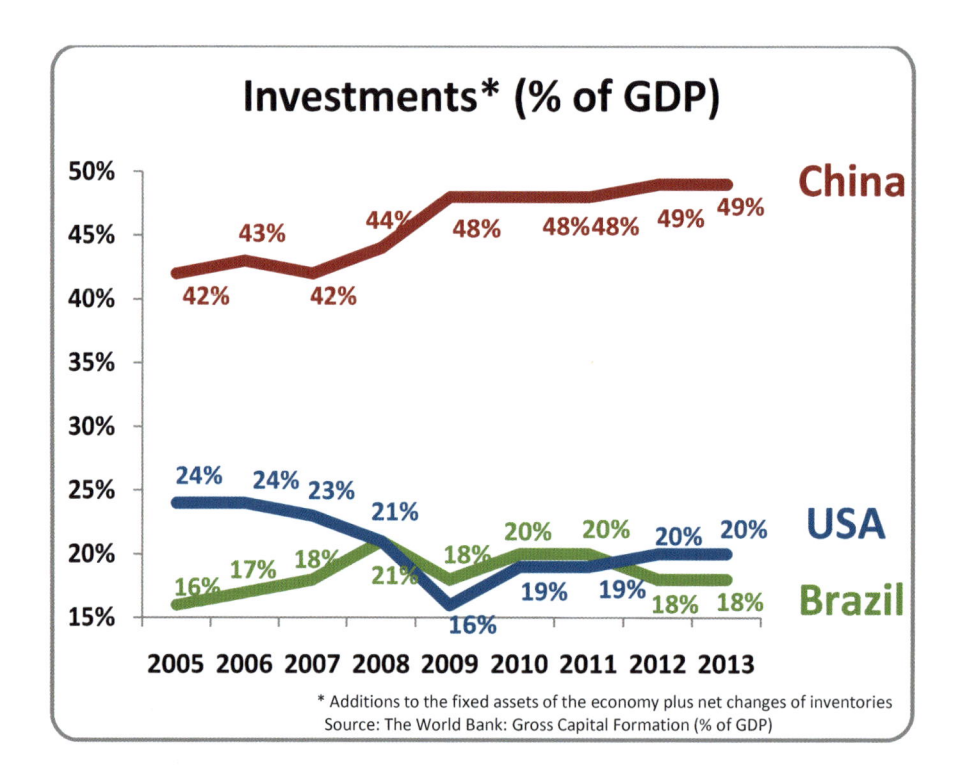

Investments* (% of GDP)

Year	China	USA	Brazil
2005	42%	24%	16%
2006	43%	24%	17%
2007	42%	23%	18%
2008	44%	21%	21%
2009	48%	16%	18%
2010	48%	18%	20%
2011	48%	19%	20%
2012	49%	19%	20%
2013	49%	20%	18%

* Additions to the fixed assets of the economy plus net changes of inventories
Source: The World Bank: Gross Capital Formation (% of GDP)

This is probably one of the most important indicators related to the Chinese phenomenon. The China investment level is the biggest in the world. The investment is crucial to the growth of any economy, and run the fundamental cycle of the growth: investment plus production and consumption equals growth.

Inflation Rate

Inflation Rate

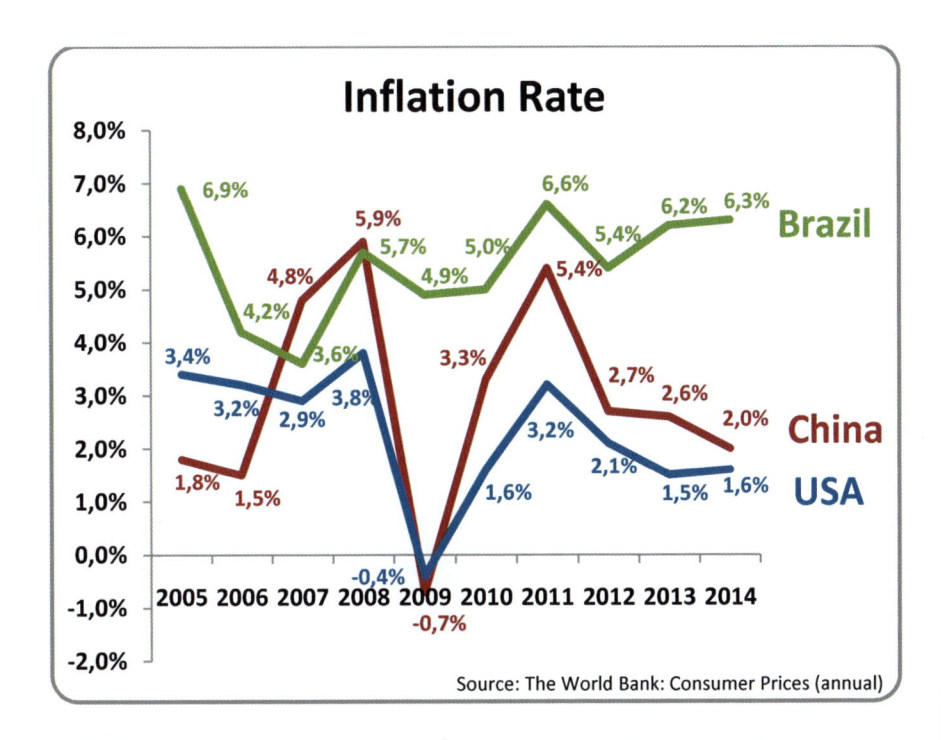

Year	Brazil	China	USA
2005	6.9%	1.8%	3.4%
2006	4.2%	1.5%	3.2%
2007	3.6%	4.8%	2.9%
2008	5.7%	5.9%	3.8%
2009	4.9%	-0.7%	-0.4%
2010	5.0%	3.3%	1.6%
2011	6.6%	5.4%	3.2%
2012	5.4%	2.7%	2.1%
2013	6.2%	2.6%	1.5%
2014	6.3%	2.0%	1.6%

Source: The World Bank: Consumer Prices (annual)

Inflation rate seems to be controlled in China and USA, but is becoming an issue in Brazil.

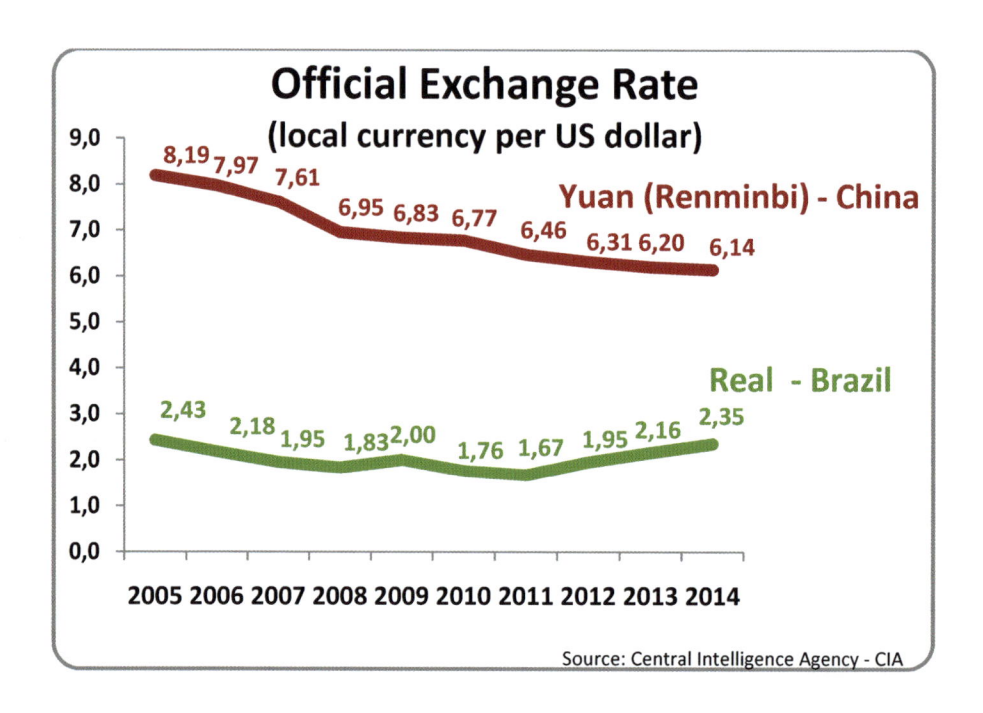

Exchange Rate

Official Exchange Rate (local currency per US dollar)

Year	Yuan (Renminbi) - China	Real - Brazil
2005	8,19	2,43
2006	7,97	2,18
2007	7,61	1,95
2008	6,95	1,83
2009	6,83	2,00
2010	6,77	1,76
2011	6,46	1,67
2012	6,31	1,95
2013	6,20	2,16
2014	6,14	2,35

Source: Central Intelligence Agency - CIA

By the official exchange rate chart, Yuan is becoming a bit stronger, every year. Considering the series showed at the chart, is about 3% raise per year. Any more could have negative impacts for the China's economy. Exporting nations benefit from a lower currency, and China is blamed of currency manipulation by keeping the currency undervalued. Obviously that this is a controversial subject, but it is important to say, as an information, that many other countries do that. Even the USA keeps the dollar low by keeping interest rates about zero (increasing credit and the money supply) and by an expansionary fiscal policy.

Trade Balance

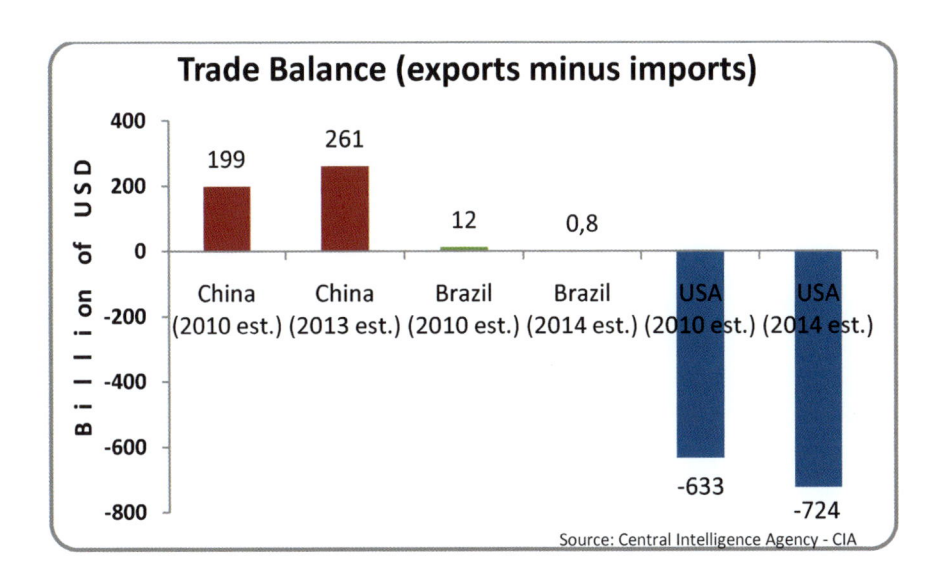

Trade Balance (exports minus imports) (Billion of USD)

- China (2010 est.): 199
- China (2013 est.): 261
- Brazil (2010 est.): 12
- Brazil (2014 est.): 0,8
- USA (2010 est.): -633
- USA (2014 est.): -724

Source: Central Intelligence Agency - CIA

The main China export partners: US 20.03%, Hong Kong 12.03%, Japan 8.32%, South Korea 4.55%, Germany 4.27% (2009). The main China import partners: Japan 12.27%, Hong Kong 10.06%, South Korea 9.04%, US 7.66%, Taiwan 6.84%, Germany 5.54% (2009).

Electricity Balance

Electricity Balance (produced minus consumed)

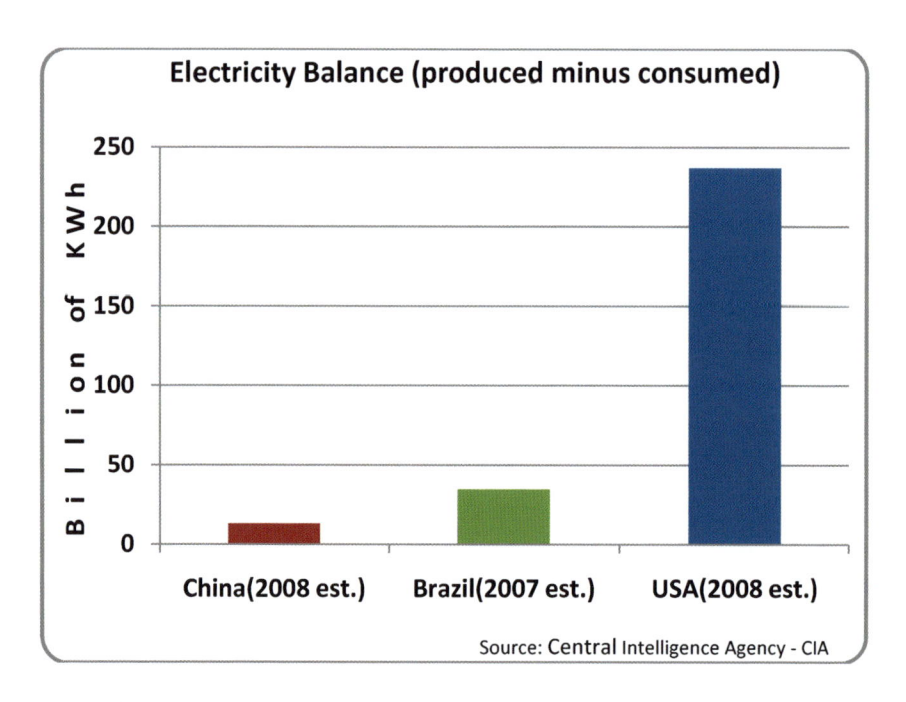

(Bar chart showing Billion of KWh for China (2008 est.) ~15, Brazil (2007 est.) ~35, USA (2008 est.) ~235)

Source: Central Intelligence Agency - CIA

China is hungry for energy and its the largest energy consumer in the world. Expand the electricity supply is one of the biggest challenges for the government. According to the CIA (2013 est.), China's biggest electricity source comes from fossil fuels (69,1%) and hydroelectric (22,5%). In USA is fossil fuel (75,3%) and nuclear fuel (9,7%). In Brazil is hydroelectric (71%) and fossil fuel (19,6%).

Energy Matrix

Energy Matrix

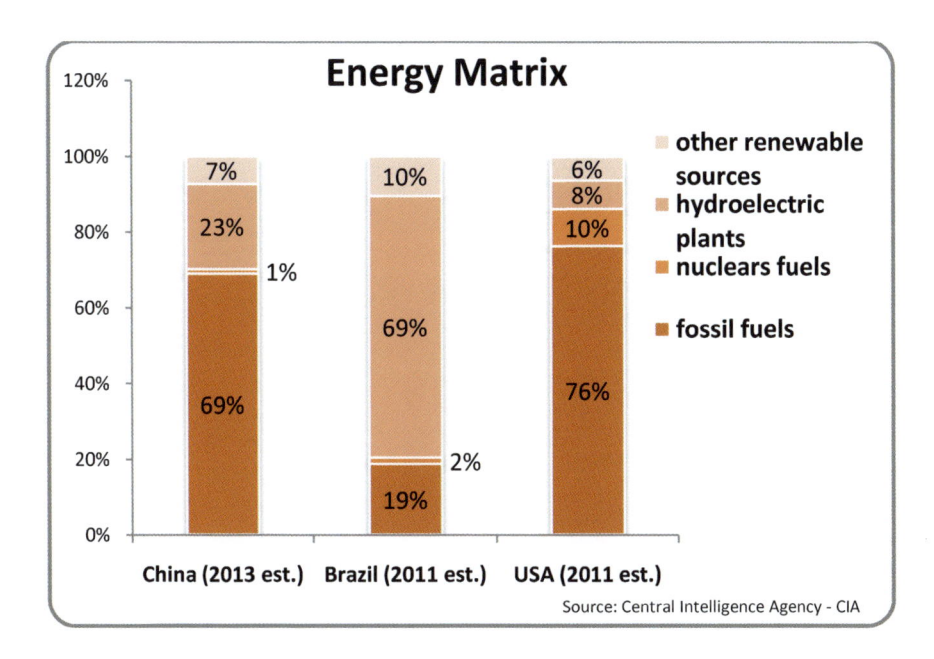

	China (2013 est.)	Brazil (2011 est.)	USA (2011 est.)
fossil fuels	69%	19%	76%
nuclears fuels	1%	2%	10%
hydroelectric plants	23%	69%	8%
other renewable sources	7%	10%	6%

Source: Central Intelligence Agency - CIA

Fossil fuels are related to pollution. USA and China has a predominance of this type of source. Brazil is concentrated in hydroelectric plants to supply energy, but is significantly exposed to the hydric crisis. It's clear that the world needs to get another kind of solution or even a more intelligent mix of energy source.

Shanghai

CHINA – The Oriental Giant   Rodrigo Vargas   43

The famous view of Pudong area (with fog) from the Bund. You can see the Oriental Pearl TV Tower in front and, behind, the Shanghai World Financial Center (the building, with the aperture on top), one of the 5 tallest buildings in the world.

The Bund seen from Oriental Pearl TV Tower, and the Huangpu River.

Shanghai Oriental Pearl Radio & TV Tower is the highest TV tower in Asia, and the third in the world, with 468 meters high. The last pearl (3rd) is 350 meters high.

JinMao Tower and Shanghai World Financial Center (with a trapezoid-shaped opening on the top) in the background. A view from Oriental Pearl TV Tower.

Shanghai World Financial Center (on the left) and Jin Mao Tower (right). The Shanghai World Financial Center was finished in 2008, with 101 floors above ground and 492 meters high. There is an observatory located at the 100 floor (474m), wich is the tallest in the world. JinMao Tower (on the right) was built in 1999, with 88 floors and reaching 421 meters. There is an observation deck on the 88th floor.

Top of JinMao Tower in front and Oriental Pearl Tower in the background. A view from the Observatory of the Shanghai World Financial Center, which is the world's highest (474m).

Shanghai view from the Shanghai World Financial Center observatory (474m).

Huangpu River. Financial area (Pudong) on the front, and the Bund on the other side of the river.

Shanghai World Financial Center building, the tallest structure in China, and one of the five tallest buildings in the world (492m).

JinMao Tower (421m), and: a bottom up view.

The Shanghai Museum shows an impressive collection of ancient Chinese art. The building has round top and a square base, symbolizing the ancient Chinese perception of the world as round sky & square earth.

The Shanghai Grand Theater.

The Nanjing Road, which is one of the world's busiest shopping street.

The Shanghai South Railway Station, Its one of two major stations in Shanghai. Extensive renovation finished in 2006.

Statue of Mao Tse Tung at The Bund.

Architecture contrasts in Shanghai.

Bus stop.

Skyscrapers in Shanghai financial area.

Skyscrapers in Shanghai financial area.

The modern Shanghai Pudong international airport.

The busy Shanghai Peoples's Square subway station.

Old commerce street in Shanghai.

Scenes From China

The rickshaw, a popular transport in China for people.

You can see all kinds of vehicles for transportation in China.

Small vehicle for transportation.

You can easily see this kind of transportation on streets.

The one on the left, in the upper side, tastes like chicken.

Typical snacks sold on streets.

Street food.

Street food.

CHINA – The Oriental Giant   Rodrigo Vargas   63

The Chinese Guardian Lions, traditionally in pairs in the entrance of buildings, they are believed to have mythic protective powers.

The Chinese Guardian Lions variation.

See the detail of the opening and closing time on the door of the pharmacy. Commerce in general also does it.

Tai Chi Chuan in the mornings.

Fair in the park.

Fair in the park.

CHINA – The Oriental Giant					Rodrigo Vargas					66

Chinese Revolution Memorial Hall, was built in 1959 in Jiaxing for the First National Congress of Communist Party, and it is considered one of the 100 classic red scenic spots in China.

Tomb-sweeping day, a holiday to honor the ancestors. Some people celebrate the day flying kites.

Shopping.

Busy streets.

Image of solar panels on top of the buildings. Extensive use in China.

Training with swords in the square.

Train station, in Jiaxing (near Shanghai).

Ancient façade in Jiaxing.

Moon River – Grand Canal. The Grand Canal is considered one of Chinese people's greatest works, like the Great Wall. It is the longest canal or artificial river in the world, from Beijing up to Hangzhou.

Moon River – Grand Canal.

Moon River – Grand Canal.

Quaint Meiwan Street, in Jiaxing. The street is so named because it is said to be a place where people planted plum trees.

Meiwan Street.

Meiwan Street.

The beauty of the scenario at Meiwan Street.

CHINA – The Oriental Giant   Rodrigo Vargas   74

Jiaxing South Lake Park.

The beauty of Chinese landscape in the Jiaxing South Lake Park.

Jiaxing South Lake Park.

Traditional Chinese architecture.

Yanyu Pavilion, on the Jiaxing South Lake, it is one of China's 8 famous buildings.

Jiaxing South Lake Park.

Jiaxing South Lake Park.

Plum trees.

Jiaxing South Lake Park.

Haogu Tower.

The Chinese Guardian Lions in the Park.

End of Trip

During my 30 days visit to China, I have known a great country and that's why I wanted to share with you a little bit of my experience, so you can learn something more about this giant country, as I did. Hopefully you have enjoyed it!

Travel to China, for business or leisure, is, certainly, a great experience!

Printed in Poland
by Amazon Fulfillment
Poland Sp. z o.o., Wrocław